PRAISE FOR **THE ATLA**

"Of all publications the Midwest Writing Center has put out, this is the most recent."
— *Lindsey Wheeler, MWC Board Administrator*

"Reading *The Atlas* will make you feel as though you made a new friend, but he is that guy who tells inappropriate stories in formal settings."
— *That Guy with the Inappropriate Stories*

"This magazine gets you where you're going, but lacks direction."
— *Cartographers Weekly*

"People may judge you for who you are, but after reading *The Atlas*, you'll feel better about yourself." — *That Emo Kid with the Sad Facial Expressions*

"This is an exemplary publication which evokes a deep sense of verisimilitude and ecstatic melancholy. While making my way through its conundrums and precarious corners, I found the work of these fine young people to be enigmatic, ostentatious, and idiosyncratic. This spontaneous reaction not being something to which I am prone to in my current referential state, I must admit I am smitten with their athletic, dexterous and intoxicating language. *The Atlas* is no exercise in floccinaucinihilipilification."
— *Merriam Webster*

"It's like watching a car crash. Although you want to, you just can't look away. Or maybe *The Atlas* is crashing into you? It's hard to tell."
— *Brian J. Krans, author of* A Constant Suicide

"There was an writing internship program going on downstairs? We had no idea. Maybe our dog was just barking." — *The Upstairs Neighbors*

"Caught up in the crossfire between poetry and prose, these young writers rebelled against the norms of literary conventions to bridge the gap between the two diverse worlds. These interns write with fire and joy in their hearts."
— *Ryan Collins, author of* Complicated Weather

Thank you for purchasing *The Atlas, Volume 5*. Inside, you will find the cure for whatever ails you. While this product has unlimited refills (or re-reads), please feel free to purchase more copies, in case you lose one or would like to pass one along to your friends or loved ones.

But, before you begin, the FDA has suggested we make you aware of the following side effects:

Before reading *The Atlas, Volume 5*, talk to your doctor. Its content may cause heartburn, pink eye, dyslexia, upset stomach, diarrhea, vomiting, insecurity, shock, indigestion, depression, and incessant giggling.

A small number of cases have reported experiencing joy, streaming tears, hair loss, shifty eyes, nostalgia, outbursts of inappropriate language, chaffing, twitching, swollen feet, cotton mouth, paranoia, hysteria, continuous blinking, and mumbling after reading The Atlas, Volume 5.

Please read as directed if you have a previous history of disbelief, teenage angst, growth spurts, change in voice, maturity, sweaty palms, stage fright, a fear of the dark, zombie confrontations, uncontrolled animal attacks, shell shock, getting lost, or writer's block.

If you and your doctor feel you are healthy enough to ingest the contents of The Atlas, Volume 5, please take a deep breath, carefully turn the page and enjoy...

Young Emerging Writers, August 2010

Notes:
"Yew and I #1 and #2" (pages 3 and 107) are centos, or poems made entirely of lines borrowed from other authors. In this case, every line in each cento is borrowed from selections in this magazine. These centos were arranged by Elisabeth Athas.

Lines 1-7 of "To One's Child" by Alyssa Young (page 78) are borrowed from the poem "Mother to Son" by Langston Hughes.

Sections of "This is Cactus Land" by Skylar Alexander (page 102) are borrowed from the poem "The Hollow Men" by T.S. Eliot.

The Midwest Writing Center is a non-profit literary arts organization committed to "fostering the appreciation of the written word, supporting and educating its creators." For information about membership, other programs, or to purchase additional copies of *The Atlas* or other MWC Press titles, please contact us:

Midwest Writing Center
Bucktown Center for the Arts
225 East 2nd Street
Davenport, IA 52801
(563) 324-1410
mwc@midwestwritingcenter.org
www.midwestwritingcenter.org

Our most sincere thanks to Fidlar Doubleday, the Melvin McKay Trust, Quad City Arts' Arts Dollar$, and the Riverboat Development Authority for their generous support of the Young Emerging Writers Internship Program and *The Atlas*.

Our love, gratitude and respect to the following: the Midwest Writing Center Board of Directors and Volunteer Staff; Lindsey Wheeler, Board Administrator; Margaret Foley, Intern; Timothy Curry, founder of the YEW Program; Thomas Moore; Katherine Beydler; and all the friends and family of the 2010 Young Emerging Writers for their support and hard work to make this program and this magazine happen.

© Midwest Writing Center Press 2010 ● Davenport, Iowa
© Route Nine Press 2010 ● Iowa Quad Cities
ISBN: #978-0-9818089-6-3
Editorial Director: Ryan Collins
Front and Back Cover Design: Thomas Moore | www.thomas-moore.net
Page Design and Interior Layout: Katherine Beydler
Printed by Fidlar Doubleday, Davenport, Iowa

Table of Contents

YEW and I #1 — All, arranged by Elisabeth Athas...3
A Letter Home — Elisabeth Athas 4
Happy the Apple — Chris Valle..5
The Graveyard — Rachel Stern...9
D D D D A D A D D D D E G Gb D — Douglas Jordan.......................................11
To the Shagflies; To the Fireflies — Skylar Alexander..12
Letters to Heart, Mind, and Soul — Jaimee Buttgen...14
And you're the bringer of this sickness — Megan Schmidt.....................................16
Little Ditty 'Bout Jack and What's Her Name — Whitney Gillum.............................19
Boyhood — Douglas Jordan...21
Blue Carpet — Katie Revelle..22
Symptoms of Loneliness — Chris Valle..23
I Drew a Smiling Face On My Bathroom Mirror — Skylar Alexander.....................24
Led On — Elisabeth Athas...25
To You Do I Blame — Logan Jawoisz..27
Trapped — Alyssa Young..28
Escaping the Pigpen — Whitney Gillum...29
The Stairs and What's Under Theres — Elisabeth Athas.......................................32
After School Special — Skylar Alexander...33
I'll set heaven on fire for you — Douglas Jordan..35
Luster, Norway — Jaimee Buttgen..36
Cherish the Memories — Logan Jawoisz...37
The Clock — Katie Revelle..38
Stimulant Series 5 — Douglas Jordan..39
You Are My Heart — Rachel Stern. 42
Salt and Pepper — Katie Revelle...43
Sylvia — Nikki Steinbaugh..44
I Just Don't Know What To Do With Myself — Jaimee Buttgen and Douglas Jordan...45
Stalker — Chris Valle..47
Discretion — Jaimee Buttgen, Rachel Stern, Megan Schmidt, Alyssa Young, Logan Jawoisz and Nikki Steinbaugh..51
A Doll Without A Heart — Megan Schmidt..52
Terminal Conversations — Katie Revelle...53
Dear Chicago — Nikki Steinbaugh..55

Dear LaSalle Street — Nikki Steinbaugh..56
Rooms — Katie Revelle...57
Smaller Questions with Bigger Answers — Elisabeth Athas..................................58
Cute as a Button — Chris Valle..59
Choose Your Reprise — Rachel Stern...63
11:14 P.M. Central Standard Time — Whitney Gillum...64
Eleven Fourteen — Douglas Jordan...67
A Game Life Plays — Alyssa Young..69
Night Walker — Jaimee Buttgen, Rachel Stern, Megan Schmidt, Alyssa Young and Nikki Steinbaugh..70
Death and Dinner — Rachel Stern..71
Waiting for Harry — Chris Valle...72
Morning People — Douglas Jordan..75
The Barracks — Jaimee Buttgen...76
And the wonder that's keeping the stars apart — Megan Schmidt........................77
To One's Child — Alyssa Young...78
Form is a father — Douglas Jordan..79
Her — Chris Valle..80
Searching for Something More — Logan Jawoisz...81
The Woods, Honey — Nikki Steinbaugh...82
Scent Memory — Elisabeth Athas..83
Dear Monrovia, — Rachel Stern...84
Response to "Reading Postures 3" — Jaimee Buttgen..85
To Someone Special — Katie Revelle..86
Silent Cries — Alyssa Young..87
I'll Walk You Home — Jaimee Buttgen..88
There is No Sound — Elisabeth Athas..90
Brother, Can I Bum a Light? — Skylar Alexander..91
No One Else Knows — Jaimee Buttgen..93
Snowfield — Megan Schmidt...94
The Current, The Lights, and Myself — Elisabeth Athas......................................97
Rebirth the Night to Day — Rachel Stern...100
This is Cactus Land — Skylar Alexander..102
YEW and I #2 — All, arranged by Elisabeth Athas..107

The Atlas
Vol. 5, Summer 2010

YEW and I #1

By finding the seams in the sky
Some are already on their way to a foreign land.
I will not lie to you,
On every street there is a businessman to point us toward
Where the heart should be but now is only hollow ground.
My friend, I am disheartened to see you torn apart,
Turning down the wrong road.
Yet she stands in the sunbeams, calling me out of my quivering.
Mostly, I try to ignore her.
There is no sound so abandoned as the sound of one's name.
To you do I blame for ruining an angelic heart.
He sipped his coffee, and she remained silent.

A Letter Home

To Fort Jackson,

    Get to everyone; some sooner and more than others. Find what makes them tick and make them tock instead. You are a master horologist; a keeper of time.

    Feel the seconds send shock waves to the tops of trees. Be the gust that goes all the way to the roots. You are awake and alive, but cannot survive.

    Not without me.

                    Semper Fi,
                        A Marine

Happy the Apple

CHRIS **VALLE**

Deep in the rural Midwest, there was an orchard owned by a reputable farming family known as the Greens. Green Orchard was famous not only for having the most delicious apples in the region, but also for its picturesque beauty. This beauty was captured in the magnificent apple trees that grew in two long, green and brown rows, speckled with warm colors. A dirt path ran between the two rows of trees. The path led all the way to the back of the orchard, all the way to a big, grassy knoll known as Sunny Hill.

On top of the hill, there was one large red apple tree. This tree was the Green family's favorite because it always produced the plumpest, juiciest fruit. The Green family took much pride in the apples that came from Sunny Hill, and even the apples themselves knew they were the best of the best. Among these proud red apples was Happy, who was as certain as every other piece of fruit hanging on the tree that she was going to be savored by someone special one day.

Happy the apple stood out as one of the most impressive fruit on her tree. She was the cream of the crop, with a perfect shape, color, and size. Every day as the sun rose over the hill, Happy shined triumphantly from the top of the tree imagining the day when she would be plucked from her branch and sent off to be tasted. Happy knew she was not the kind of apple that would be skinned and put into pies or ground up into cider. She was much too pretty for that sort of thing. She was the kind of apple that would be appreciated all on her own.

One bright, warm morning, Happy's daydreaming was interrupted by murmurs from her neighbors, Round and Red.

"Did you hear about Lumpy?" One said to the other.

"Lumpy? What happened to him?"

"He fell Down Below."

"Oh, no!"

"We should've known he could not last with his shape."

Happy had heard hushed gossip of this nature before. There were always whispers of "Down Below" when an apple started to spoil a little. The gossip continued to grow as the harvest approached.

"Did you hear about Seedy?"

"Seedy? What happened to her?"

"She had a hole."

"A hole? Oh no!"

"Now she too has gone Down Below."

Talk of Down Below always disturbed Happy's naturally content nature, even though an apple of her quality was not the type who would end up there. Happy tried to ignore the petty gossip of the other apples.

As the sun was setting one late summer evening, Happy was startled by a voice calling to her.

"Happy! Happy!"

"Oh, hello, Worm."

"Wow, you are looking great, Happy. Mr. Green might even keep you for himself."

Happy blushed, although Worm would never be able to tell because of Happy's naturally red hue.

Happy had always enjoyed talking to Worm. She appreciated having some company that wasn't caught up in apple gossip.

As the two looked out over the scarlet sunset, Happy said to Worm "I really enjoy talking to you. It feels good to hear about something new. I am so sick of hearing about Down Below."

"Down Below?" Worm said casually. "Down Below is not so bad."

"You've been there?" Happy was quite surprised.

"Why, of course. I am a worm after all."

"Oh... right."

Happy was only vaguely familiar with what the life of a worm was like. She really only understood the lives of apples, and maybe trees.

Worm visited Happy the next three afternoons. Happy was thankful to have someone to keep her company while she eagerly waited for the harvest.

"You must be one of the prettiest apples in this whole tree, Happy."

"Thank you, Worm. Did you notice how the leaves on this tree aren't as thick as they were? I bet this tree is going to change colors soon."

"Could be." Worm did not take his beady eyes off of Happy. "You really look delicious. Farmer Green is going to gobble you all up."

"Thank you, Worm," Happy said growing slightly uncomfortable with all of the flattery.

"Happy, would you mind if I had just a little taste?"

Happy's leaves curled with tension. "I don't know, Worm."

"Well, I could tell you for certain if you were the most delicious apple on this tree."

"Really?"

"Oh, yes. Most of the quality apples have me check their progress every once in a while. That's what worms are here for."

"Oh, in that case, help yourself, Worm."

"Good choice, Miss Happy. Good choice."

Worm did not hesitate for even a moment. Happy cringed with pain as Worm punctured her ripe, red skin.

"Now bear with me, Happy. This may hurt a little."

As Worm pushed his way deeper into the nervous apple's body, Happy felt pressure build up uncomfortably inside her. She whimpered a little as Worm ate away at her insides.

"Worm, please. You said just a little." Already Happy was regretting her decision.

After just a few more delicious bites, Worm oozed his way out of Happy and slipped back down on to the branch beside her.

"I think you're quite delicious," said Worm after a long silence.

Happy looked down at the ugly hole in her body with shame. "Please go away, Worm."

Eventually, the brisk wind blew the autumn across the orchard. By that time, the hole in Happy's body had only grown more hideous. The skin around the hole had begun to curl inwards. Her once firm and juicy insides had began to discolor and turn soggy. Of course, this ugliness was unbearably humiliating for poor little Happy, especially with her gossiping neighbors. However, this was far from the worst of Happy's problems. Every night, Happy would weep in pain as soreness and sogginess spread through her entire body.

"Have you seen Happy lately?" Round said to Red one morning.

"Happy? How is she?"

"She has a hole. You didn't see?"

"A hole? Oh no!"

"We know where she'll go."

With little time left before the harvest, Happy was barely hanging on to her branch. She had heard what the other fruit had been saying about her. She knew she was no longer the pretty apple she once was. Certain there was no chance she could turn over a new leaf, Happy let go of her branch and descended to Down Below.

Sitting at the bottom of the tree where she never thought she'd be, Happy said quietly to herself, "At least there is still green grass down here."

Days passed and Happy's inside turned almost entirely to mush. As

Happy was wallowing in her defeat, she saw Worm pass by. "Worm."

"Oh, hello Happy. Fancy seeing you down here." Worm tried to avoid making eye contact.

"I used to be all the way at the top of the tree, Worm," she said. "But now I'm just another rotten apple Down Below."

"It's not so bad down here."

Finally, the harvest arrived. Farmer Green brought a bushel up Sunny Hill early one autumn morning, ready to pick all of the pretty apples from his favorite tree. In spite of everything, Happy grew hopeful. Maybe Mr. Green would recognize her for the apple she once was. Maybe he'd forgive that ugly hole in her, admiring her for the perfect shape she used to possess.

With hopeful eyes, Happy gazed up to the top of the tree. Her thoughts wandered to a time when she was ripe, red, and beautiful. A time before she had a disgusting, gaping hole in her body. The sun stung her eyes a little as she stared up into the leaves.

It was the last thing she saw before the farmer's boot came down upon her.

The Graveyard

I like to go down to the graveyard and wonder.

The gates scrape open and
rows of stone stretch out before me,
a farm where nothing grows.

An Iris tumbles past my feet.
They are not in season, but
I bend to save it from another gust.

I like to lie in front of a name and date, body matching body.

My hand runs over the dewy grass
where the heart isn't
and I wonder.

What I would give for a chat
with the stones,
a trip under the heavy dirt.

I could feel the flowers growing up between my joints
roots tickling my cheek
earth slowly eroding my existence.

I can taste the darkness,
hear the absence.
I am drunk with death, one with soil.

But the wind gusts and
I find that my heart is still full
and theirs is not.

I like to listen as the wind tears through the graveyard.

I take the Iris
and place it over where the heart should be
but now is only hollow ground.

An American flag whips against a pole
and the sun at half-mast
does not reach farther than the grass.

D D D A D A D D D D E G Gb D

DOUGLAS JORDAN

"123" She counted the petals as they kissed the ground before her. An even number, he loves her. An odd number results in a normal outcome: heartbreak and disappointment. "123" His obsession with Jim Morrison and Jack White had its baggage: a haunting obsession with the number 3. Combined with his love of piano and all 7th chords are unplayable by his fingers. He wrote her part of a song the night before. She may never hear it, and that's perfectly fine with him. He continues counting his steps in a 3 beat measure. "123" and he loves me not. Maybe so, but perhaps nay. He's an odd boy and I'm a foreign exchange student from Amsterdam. He's walking this way, sure, but what could he want with a simple Dutch girl?, she ponders. Tempting fate, she picks up another tulip. "123" and I'm almost there. Almost to the first date. Almost to the I do. Almost to the happily ever after. Almost to the American Dream. Count your steps. Don't forget to breathe. Almost to the simple Dutch girl. Maybe I'll get to live in a windmill, he ponders. "123" 4.. 5.. 6.. 7.. 8.. 9.. 10. With each passing breath he draws closer. With each passing breath, she counted another stillbirth buried in Mrs. Miner's backyard. She found comfort in knowing these potential children died before being raised by that wretched old shrew. She thought of their free-choice being washed away by baptism. Confirmation was the confirmation that the last nail was in the coffin. And he's here... "123" Check if you like me, check if you don't. Check if you'll date me, check if you... "123" She was once told actions speak louder than words.
                              This is no different. *Impact*.

To the Shagflies; to the Fireflies

To the Moth, forever less than the butterfly,
The beauty long coming
And fluttering in my stomach.

To the Shagflies, knowing the shortness
Of their life spans
Seizing the day like there's no tomorrow.

To the Walking Stick, my companion
Singing, "lean on me"
As I take one final walk up the hill.

To the Cockroaches, those resilient pests
Scum of the earth
Surviving even the atom bomb.

To the Millipede, with its million arms to hug with
Hiding in dark corners
Never getting the chance to spread the love.

To the Fireflies, dipped in nuclear waste
Painting phosphorescent glow
Across the rolling midnight landscape.

To the Cicada, for personifying the world is cyclical
And summer noise is symphony
For teaching us everything comes back, eventually.

To the Daddy Long Legs, mistaken for spiders
When they're not
With their fangs as harmless as senile old men.

To the Lady Bugs—even the poor, misguided male ones.
Trying to find themselves
In a world overrun with copycat beetles.

To the Grasshopper, for mastering kung fu
When no one thought they could
And yet, Aesop's grasshopper still starves.

Letters to Heart, Soul, and Mind

Dear Heart,

A loyal companion thou hast been whilst I try my hand at; whilst dipping my feet in; whilst... I fail to maintain your safety. The glue solution I recommended, I'm afraid was frail, its job it did not master. My friend, I am disheartened to see you torn apart, strewn about as though you were a puzzle someone has left undone. You deserve to shine, to glisten like a masterpiece, radiating with beams from all regions. The troubled times you have endured astound me over again. I hope the rugged burns left behind, will diminish with time. Although you too are impartial, I see thy potential in the future figurine you can be.

To picking up the pieces,

    Soul

Dear Soul,

I appreciate your love for me and stuff but I just hurt so much, all the time. I mean there I am, scattered all over the floor like marbles, parts of me getting lost under the couch or the rug, or that one time that boy accidently stepped on a piece. Ugh. Talk about kicking me while I was down. I know you try your best but, honestly? I think I quit. Love hurts too much. It's tough and brutal and stings way too long. You tell me that I'll get better with time. Well, maybe I should be sending Time a little note too, telling him to hurry up, because right now I hate how this feels. Please try to do better this time.

I'm waiting for better glue,

    Heart

Dear Heart and Soul,

    I am sorry to intervene with such a blunt intrusion but I am afraid I cannot be privy to this pathetic situation any longer. I would like to take this time to address both of you as I feel it necessary to do so.

    Soul, to start I am disappointed in the weak attempts you have provided in saving Heart's stability. I believe that if greater endeavors or a proclamation had been made directed to me then I would have been guided to the situation. I am positive I could have helped oversee the security of Heart and we would not be in such a quandary. Next time I hope you would coordinate a better plan.

    Heart, please, try to grow up? A little bit of maturity and maybe even a sense of how you truly feel may help eliminate some of these obstructions. I do not have much to say to you seeing as you are incapable of comprehending formal speech during your current state of, well, shall I say, your depression. I am sorry you are again in pain. I hope that you and Soul will better inform me next time and I can intervene sooner.

Hoping your next solution doesn't involve glue,

        Mind

And you're the bringer of this sickness

MEGAN SCHMIDT

It's evening, and I'm not in crazytown yet. This is worthy of celebration.

I'm making a cup of tea—chamomile for calm, I repeat it to myself—when the first pinpricks of misgiving crawl up my neck. My nerves are jittery. I can't concentrate and burn myself spilling the water. Something, I think, is crawling around the eaves of this house, seeking out the smell of my flesh.

I set my cup of tea on the coffee table. There is a documentary on the television, something about the Hoover Dam, but I can't concentrate on it. I walk carefully to the front door in its little alcove, unlock it, and look outside. The porch light illuminates the stoop, making my shadow grow long. When I'm satisfied that no one is pressing themselves up against the wall, waiting for me to fall asleep so they can bust down the door, I close it again and lock it.

Just to be safe, I wedge a heavy box of books against it so it can't open, then go to check the kitchen windows and the back door. I pull the curtains and latch them, then return to my tea. It's cold. In the sink it goes. I don't bother with a new cup, and instead extricate a smashed water bottle from the fridge.

I curl into the sagging couch. It's ugly and green, but it has the careful familiarity of things past their time, so I keep it. My muscles are aching from the constant tension. A bath would help with that, I suppose. The narrator's voice is a constant, grating drone, and it doesn't even provide a semblance of relaxing background noise. I turn it off and begin the pre-bedtime ritual circuit of the house.

The first room is the bathroom. No one is lying in the bathtub or crouching in the cabinet under the sink. The window, high up on the wall, has no ladder leaning against the house beneath it. Latching that window, I close the door and check the linen closet. It's empty as well, so I move onto the guest bedroom. The closet is empty, and no one is beneath the bare bed. There's nothing in the room but the bed and a table, with one lowly shoebox in the closet anyways, so there wouldn't be much place for someone to hide, I suppose. With that room clear, I walk downstairs to the small basement. It's mostly empty as well, save for the washer and dryer and a few boxes. I lock the door when I head upstairs and finally go to my room.

My room is the only place with any sort of clutter. I reach beneath my

DOMESTIC BLISS QC

Handmade and repurposed or upcycled vintage furnishings and décor for individuals who are looking for high-quality products with an artistic feel.

Visit our new store opening in June in Rock Island's newly renovated SHOPPES ON 2ND

1700 2nd Avenue Suite 5

Rock Island

We offer a unique variety of retail products from many QC artisans with a focus on handmade, upcycled, and eco-friendly items. Additionally, we carry an eclectic mix of vintage and new items including home and office decor, furniture, gifts, accessories, and more.

Present this flyer for 10% off any purchase of $25 or more

bed and push aside all of the boxes beneath it before I'm satisfied that no one has managed to fit themselves under it. Rifling through the sundresses and sweaters in the closet, I find no one. There isn't any living being save a lady bug beneath my desk. I sigh in relief and lock the door, and then sit on my desk, confident that nobody will grab my ankles.

Flicking on the wheezing computer, I sip my water. I'm supposed to type up the historical society newsletter. I've spent the past two years of my life dedicated to this failing group, and it almost gave me some peace, an anchor to a past that wasn't mine, but now I'd rather not have anything to do with it, after tonight.

I still have to get it done, though. At least all that's left is to type up the names. Mine is first. Robin Almassy. Move down the list. Dave Barlow. Jacob Ebner. Michelle Feldt.

With the list of fourteen names done, I tie up the newsletter with a cheery note—All are welcome to join the society! And don't forget, donations are always welcome! I save it and turn off the computer.

I yank a brush through the snarls in my hair. I don't care about brushing my teeth, no one will see me in the morning anyway. I flick on the children's nightlight I own before turning off my lamp and curling hurriedly into bed.

The light glows behind Princess Aurora. I wish a dashing prince would come out of Disney and sweep me off to fairytale land. Maybe I could try to find my fairy godmother. Maybe her number's in the phone book.

I shut my eyes tight. He was here today, enemy number one, at the museum. I'd been working the morning shift, and He sauntered in, holding the hand of his daughter. Smile on his face like always, as if nothing had ever happened, like we were still friends.

"Been a while since I've seen you, I thought you moved or something," He'd told me, sliding across the money for admission. I didn't answer, giving him a crazy-eyed look instead.

Then off He went around the museum, his daughter looking at the displays with wide eyes. I ducked my head over inventory and tried not to look at him. It would be nice to turn into a pot and shatter into pieces. I could be added to the case with the rest of them: bits of ancient Africa and Asia, Europe and America.

I open my eyes again. I can almost feel his presence, pushing out the air I breathe. It feels like a heart attack.

I sit up. It's too cold. After braving the hallway to fiddle with the knob to turn the temperature down, I resign myself to the air conditioning being broken.

Will insurance cover that? Probably not. Insurance sucks.

I can't find my quilt either, and so I curl up on my bed, knees to my chest, a fleece blanket draped around my shoulders.

Maybe my fairy godmother would have a spell to help people like me. I bet that old gravy tureen is actually Aladdin's lamp. I ponder briefly what I would say if the Genie actually showed up. I know you're big and blue and kind of ugly and I never liked you, but can I have three wishes?

The tree that nearly eclipses my house scrapes against the siding. Despite the late hour, I can hear the tired old man who lives across the street dragging his garbage can up from the curb. Someone is pulling into their driveway. I think there's a squirrel in my wall, because I can hear chittering and scampering. That will keep me up all night in cold sweats. Something else insurance won't cover.

That a squirrel could get into the wall concerns me. If a squirrel can exploit that weakness, a person certainly can. I guess I need to call the landlord. I pull my blanket up to my chin and try to focus on the chores I need to do tomorrow, instead of the stagnant memories He brought in his wake.

Maybe I'd do better in Oz instead of Disney. I could be cowardly with the Lion, and sleep for a while in the Emerald City. I bet block parties on the Yellow Brick Road get pretty wild.

It's no use. The ghostly feeling of a hand on my thigh, of breaking in half, of trying to get him off of me, off of my bed, persists.

I hang my head over my knees, dig my sharp fingernails into the skin stretched over my hand. I can't breathe. I still think it's that day, that night. Nothing is ever safe. Nothing is ever free.

It is still August. The sun will still be burning tomorrow. But a December of two years ago swirls in my head and all around my shoulders, until the fear of it makes me wish that something—maybe a tornado, maybe the coming of Christ—could take it away.

Little Ditty 'Bout Jack and What's Her Name

WHITNEY GILLUM

Outside the large windows, planes flew in every direction. Some were coming, some were going, some already on their way to a foreign land. He watched them, waiting nervously. She should have arrived nearly an hour ago, and he hadn't gotten news of any delays. Maybe she changed her mind, he thought. What if she decided he just wasn't worth it anymore? He shook his head, attempting to free his mind of the troubling thoughts. It didn't work. He began to pace, the flowers in his hand falling to his side as his shoulders drooped.

"Jack!" a voice called.

He snapped his head to the direction of the voice. He had heard his name, but where was she?

"Jack!" the voice yelled again with a laugh. He spotted a red haired girl running towards another man before jumping into his open arms. He sighed. Giving another glance out to the crowded terminal, he admitted defeat. She had given up on him. Tossing the flowers into a nearby trashcan, he zipped up his jacket and made his way out of the building without a second glance. If she was done with him, he was done with her.

Jack had always known he wasn't worth it. He had gone after her since the first time he met her during freshman year of high school. He was nerdy and didn't have many people to hang around with and stayed up half the night on the internet. She wasn't popular by any means, but she was still well liked and always busy on a Saturday night. They were close friends that year and the next. She helped him break out of his shell, and eventually he gained enough courage to ask her out. Their relationship became strained when she moved across state to go to college.

One day, out of pure impulse, she drove across state to see him. He didn't know; she never called to tell him. When she got there, she was the surprised one. Jack acted like he didn't know her. In front of his friends, he was considered single, so he could mess around freely, and with a girl so far away, who would know any better? She left him that day. He would call. She wouldn't answer. He would visit. She would lock him out. He would write with no response. She didn't want him anymore. It took him almost a year to get through to her and explain himself. Even then, she didn't want to listen, but the sound of his voice pulled her in. They talked for a while before reconciling. She made plans to fly out the following week to visit him, so they could talk face to face.

***

    Where is he, she wondered as she sat on a bench outside of the bus station. She was positive she had told him she would be traveling by bus and not plane because of her fear of heights, but now she wasn't so sure. Had he forgotten? He said he would be here, she thought. It was almost night, and the station had started to empty out. Fearing she would have to spend the night there, she pulled out her phone to call him. After a ring or two, his voicemail picked up. She looked at her phone; he had ignored her call after only 14 seconds.

Putting the phone back to her ear she said, "I don't know what happened. Maybe you forgot, maybe you just didn't care. But I've been waiting for over an hour here for you to show up. 'Here' meaning the bus station." She paused, closing her eyes as tears formed, "Anyway…it's obvious you don't want to see me, so I'll just go home. I'm done waiting for you, Jack. Goodbye."

Boyhood

I thought I saw Superman twice yesterday, the first time it was a bird, the second time it was a plane. While I was out pretending to be Superman, my dad told me to give up boyhood behavior, because that's what men do. He told me to be a man and shoot our next meal. Boys pretend to be superheroes while men shoot guns.

I wish he'd remember that I never said I ever wanted to be a man. He stepped out for some chewing tobacco the next week. I haven't seen him since. He's probably out being a man and shooting things. Meanwhile, I have to be a superhero to feed me and my mom.

Blue Carpet

I had my very own space for two years. The carpet was blue for the boy my parents never had and I came into the world silently screaming. They named me for a song and placed me in that room, wallpaper littered with images of balloons.

I've always hated balloons.

My father worked all day while my mother rearranged the house daily out of missing him, playing "Strawberry Wine" by Deanna Carter and *ER* reruns that I can still quote.

But she never touched my space. I hid up there arranging my toys in order to be just like her, pretending that blue carpet was a sea I could drown in.

I remember the last day my mother and I allowed all the space my father left temporarily vacant come between us. Her overworked, sweating body folded into the couch as she watched her daily *ER* and I sat upstairs in that sea I was drowning in.

Hours passed.

Hospital records and diagnoses drifted carelessly to my room. Every operation procedure from that show shot directly to me.

Suddenly, it stopped. Harsh silence was interrupted by my mother's Bix-racer footsteps.

"Are you okay?" Her breathy voice embraced my ears. "I wasn't sure... you haven't made a sound...I was just checking..."

I lay aside the book I was reading and ran to hug her.

"No, Mommy, I'm fine."

"Come sit with me a while," she said.

And so I did.

For the next fifteen years.

Symptoms of Loneliness

Check all that apply:
___Talking excessively to your cat
___Paging through old yearbooks every night
___Waiting hours for notifications on Facebook
___Returning your parents' phone calls
___Making trips to Walmart over one insignificant item
___Dressing up to dine in alone
___Feeling overeager to greet your co-workers
___Increased hours devoted to sitcoms aimed at a younger age group
___Weighing yourself over three times per day
___Dragging out small talk with fast food employees and shop clerks
___Phone calls from telemarketers excite you
___Frequently reading your cell phone contacts list
___Dropping your car keys to see if anyone picks them up for you
___Watching teen movies from the '80s over five times in one week
___Rehearsing how you would introduce yourself to a mirror
___Calling the customer satisfaction 1-800 numbers on your household products
___Offering to help people carry their groceries
___Spying on your neighbors with binoculars
___Higher intake of ice cream each day
___Spending hours rereading the TV guide
___Leaving the television or radio on just for the sounds of voices
___Washing your clothes at the Laundromat when it isn't necessary
___Reading celebrity gossip magazines
___Carrying out extended conversations with your car
___Waiting for the mailman
___Crying when you come home to find "0 New Messages" on your answering machine
___Spending less of your paychecks
___Doing crosswords
___Improvising songs about your daily routine
___Dreaming about your exes

Result: You still miss him.

I Drew a Smiling Face On My Bathroom Mirror

I drew a smiling face on my bathroom mirror
Then it started crying.

I planted a garden, but all I could focus on was
The dirt under my nails.

I threw a party, with the trimmings perfect
Then a balloon burst.

I went picnicking with you, but all I could see was
The raincloud on the horizon.

I went to church, and had communion
Then I spilled the wine.

The plot was great, but all I could focus on was
The slipshod acting.

I went to the mall, and tried on dresses for fun
Then I looked in the mirror.

The ring's on my finger, but all I can see is
Her.

Led On

"How long can we hold on?"

"Long enough."

Her hand caught on his arm as she stumbled over the dips in the ground. He grabbed her arm and shoved her away. His pace didn't change.

"Do you even know where we're going?" she pushed.

"Where I am led."

"There is no one leading you!"

He stopped and pivoted to face her. She meant to stare back into his eyes, but found that she couldn't. She stared off to his side.

"There's somewhere we have to be for the resistance. There is no road, nor any path. Everything is hidden just like you were in that godforsaken shack. I don't know exactly where they are, but they will find us before we find them once we're close. They'll be watching for me. I don't have time for you but I wasn't going let you die. There's enough of that, so shut your mouth and keep moving."

She swore at his shadow when he continued. She'd been trailing after his steps for thirty days. When the war began he had found her and asked her name. He never told her his, but he told her to come with him. He had a blade and more than enough force, should he need to use it. She didn't argue. She wasn't leaving anything behind. There was nothing to leave behind.

The soldiers used to stand for what was right. From their hearts they would cry, "Live Free or Let Me Die." That wasn't so long ago. The soldiers invaded her home on Sunday. There was something different about the way they yelled for her family to come outside. Their words were gruff and biting. They didn't wait. Her family watched the bolts on the door spring from the wall. Even the sun forced itself through the cracks.

"Run, Schuyler," her father whispered.

She was too scared to run, so she hid. She cringed at the crack from the pistol's ignition. Most people didn't live long enough to notice the moist thud of the bullet entering the body, but when she heard it, she tasted blood. There were scars on her hand from where she had bit down to keep from screaming.

When he found her, he said they would be protected, but she didn't know who could protect them. There was hardly anyone left, much less someone that could protect them. Food was scarce and any fresh water source was controlled by the soldiers.

Still, she believed what he said. She squinted her eyes against the sun and kicked at the rocks as she kept walking.

To You Do I Blame

For it is nothing, but one.
One person, one action, one word.
Everything ever built up gets knocked down, shot to hell.

For it is nothing, but two.
Two lips, two rumors, two pieces.
Any reputation made, shattered in a single breath.

For it is nothing, but three.
Three tears, three thoughts, three scars.
The fresh skin that lay upon her arm, torn apart.

You are the ridicule, the lies, the pain.
Flooding an innocent heart.
Tormenting harmless thoughts.

To you do I blame for the gun to her head,
For the hell you put her through,
For ruining an angelic heart.

And to me do I blame for entering her life too late.
To hear her screams and tears,
Only after she had already made up her mind.

Trapped

Distorted anger
Will leave a wounded bird blind
Trapped and tormented.

Escaping the Pigpen

Everyday I walk the same halls. I see the same people. I hear the gossip as it floats its way through from one little brat to the next. My routine never alters in any way. It's not that I have a problem with change; it just makes things easier when you fall into a routine, at least, when you're like me. Since I pass by these same people, I assume they do the same. I could tell you a lot about my fellow high schoolers. I could tell you "Emily totally, like, passed out drunk, like, at a party," when really she had a bad reaction to her allergy meds, and how "Oh em gee, Miranda is, like, totes prego. What a slut!" when in reality it was her twenty-four year old, married sister.

It's impossible not to adore the problems at this hellhole I could probably go on for hours, even days, with the nonsensical crap I hear. Not a single person notices when I walk by though.. Not one. I'm alone in a sea of people. Sometimes I feel like I shouldn't be here, like I don't belong anywhere. It's like I'm Patrick Swayze in that one movie, except no one has been kind enough to let me talk to them, let alone through them. Yep, that was my attempt at a joke. If it was as awful for you to read as it was for me to write, I apologize.

The thing with me is, while everybody else is off talking about who did who and who smokes what, I'm only a few steps away with my nose buried in a book. I don't associate with people because I don't like people. Maybe once they were worth my time but not anymore. I have one more year in this place, and then I'm free. One more year and they will be long lost memories. I remember freshman year being the start of it all. It was when I thought they were good, trustworthy people. Friends even. That's all bull. People are like termites. They eat you whole until you're nothing but an empty space where your ghost resides.

Why is it we put our trust into one person? I don't understand why someone would give that to a person who could care less. I mean, I did that, and I still don't know the answer. Well, maybe I do. Everyone on this planet craves love and by trusting someone it's like they have it, but they really don't. All of it is lies and broken promises neatly hidden behind a fake smile and an insincere persona.

Now you're probably wondering what happened. I don't think you'll believe me when I tell you, but I will. Freshman year, 2007, first semester. I was "best friends" with…her. Mindy Monroe. She always told people she had a connection to, "yes, Marilyn; we're distant cousins!" I still wonder if she knows Marilyn Monroe died almost forty-eight years ago. Maybe she does but is following in dear ol' Mare's footsteps of being a "dumb blonde." Either way, she's an idiot. But this idiot knew how to get to people, how to dig deep inside and tear someone into little pieces. I should know; I was her only target.

She befriended me in our ninth grade English class within the second week of August, when school began. She had friends. I didn't. Good thing nothing's changed, right? Sorry, lame joke again. I had fallen into a depression earlier in the summer, causing me to put on nearly thirty five pounds. I had begun to feel insecure about it when I recovered, so when Mindy decided I was her best friend, well, it felt wonderful. I was wanted. Now I know what for.

As I said, this may not sound like the truth, but if you haven't figured it out, I'm not too keen on lying. Let me set the scene: December 18th, 2007. There wasn't much happening that night. It was nearing nine o'clock, and I was in the kitchen, happy to throw away my last bottle of pills. My parents were working the night shift, which had become almost routine. We needed the money for my therapy bills. I didn't mind having the house to myself, so it never really bothered me when they were out. With the bottle in the trash I smiled in triumph and made my way over to the cabinet to grab something quick to eat. There was a sound behind me, but I never bothered turning around, thinking it was just one of my two dogs running into the door again. Suddenly, a hand was covering my mouth, and my hands were pulled behind my back. I flailed around, but that only resulted in me being pushed to the ground. I rolled over onto my back and was absolutely horrified at who I saw.

"Mindy?" I shrieked, before I was silenced with tape.

"Sorry for this, deary, but playtime is over." she laughed as I started hyperventilating. Shortly after, I passed out.

I woke up shivering, surrounded by hay and a burning stench. I attempted to sit up, but found I couldn't move my arms or legs. They had my arms tied behind my back and my feet bound. Panicking, I tried to loosen the knots. My attempt was to no avail. I managed to calm myself down enough to take in my surroundings. Short walls blocked off a small area of what looked like a barn. In the middle of it, straight across from me, was a pink sleeping animal. Right then I realized exactly where I was: a pigpen.

Time passed by slowly before a man came in. At first he walked right passed me. I made a sound in the back of my throat, which caught his attention enough to make him stop walking. He turned his head in my direction when I made the sound again. The look on his face was both of horror and bewilderment. The man ran over to me and removed the tape ever so gently, then started on the rope. He kept asking me questions, like what my name was and how I got there and who did would do such a thing. I should have responded, but the rage in me made it hard to think straight. The only thing I said to him was my address. He dropped me off and told me to not do anything stupid, to be the bigger person. I never thought his words would stick with me a few years later.

From that day on I swore to myself I wouldn't get close to anyone. I wouldn't let my guard down and be crushed like I was back then. She had humiliated me so severely, it only made me loathe all of mankind. Even now, she'll walk by me and snort, trying to be funny. I ignore her. If I stooped to her level I'd have no respect for myself. I'm just waiting for the day karma comes around to slap her in the face.

"Did you hear?" a brunette sitting in front of me whispered to her friend.

"Hmm?"

I took a moment away from my book to focus on their conversation. Eavesdropping should be my middle name. I do it so well.

"Mindy Monroe? She was expelled."

"Finally! What did she do?"

"She was in chemistry working on a project and some chick walked by and accidentally bumped into her, so she threw the Sulfuric acid in the girl's face."

"That's it?"

"It completely scorched her face! I heard her mom is pressing charges!"

I smiled with a roll of my eyes. Maybe it was an exaggeration, but if so, it was the best exaggeration I've ever heard.

The Stairs and What's Under Theres

There is no place for my childhood to fit.
Where am I to put it?

Under the stairs?
It won't fit theres!

Inside the cupboard?
It's full of moof and flupboard!

I just don't know what to do.
It's not like a kazoo.

It's no playful song and dance,
And it's nothing like a crabrance!

It's much bigger than a sock,
Yet still smaller than a ferflock.

It doesn't step like a heel.
It gallops like a wondzeal!

My childhood is something I'll set aside,
Because one day I'll leave it behind.

I've this cardboard box and me,
we are looking to be free.

And we've got someone to help us,
He'll even carry the guggleruss!

He'll take the things from under the stairs,
The moof and flupboard that won't fit theres,

And He'll know exactly what to do!

He'll cradle my childhood up so tight,
And He'll walk me through this glorious light.

He'll be my everlasting guide,
To give my childhood grace and my future pride.

After School Special

"So I was reading this article in *Rolling Stone*, right?" Piper posed as she pulled her tank top down over her head. "An interview with Omar bin Laden."

A slight, disappointed sigh puttered past Alan's lips as her breasts disappeared, but he was consoled by the nipples still at attention through her shirt. "Oh?"

"Yeah. He's a total nutjob, just like daddy," she said, and then laughed. "You'd probably like him."

He smirked as he fumbled with his belt. "Probably."

After tugging her skinny jeans up her shapeless hips, she crawled across the bed between them. Shaking her short, sex-touseled hair away from her face, she poked Alan in the gut. "Have you talked to Liza yet?"

"Not yet," the man admitted, sighing as he ran a hand through his graying hair.

"She doesn't know it's me you're seeing, right?" Piper asked, her eyes serious.

"No. She just knows I'm with a younger woman." He glanced over Piper's lithe, youthful frame. "A much younger woman."

"But not a student," Piper surmised, perfectly-shaped eyebrow raised. "Not your student."

Alan hung his head and nodded. Piper had always been exceedingly bright.

"I'll leave the magazine on the kitchen table," she announced as she lazily fastened his shirt. "I'll help myself to some orange juice, if you don't mind?"

Alan's fingers, hairy and stubby in his middle-age, fumbled with the button on her jeans. "Fine. Take whatever you want, so long as you—"

"—Leave out the back door." Piper recited his words as if they were a lesson memorized in grade school. "I know, I know."

"Piper, what sort of educator would I be if I didn't constantly shove the same shit down your throat everyday August til May?" he joked.

Absentmindedly, the young girl's hands wandered south of his waistband, licking her teeth in a way that was both innocent and seductive. "Mr. P, you've been shoving the same thing down my throat since—"

"Piper!" he cried, grabbing her wrists before she could do any more

SKYLAR **ALEXANDER**

damage.

"I know, I know," she sighed with a smile, slipping her hands free and slipping them around his waist. "No more dirty jokes."

Alan eyed her sternly for several moments before his face split into a grin. Then he kissed her.

"Now, get to class, young lady," he ordered.

"Yeah, yeah," the girl whined, sighing dejectedly as she climbed out of bed. She paused in the doorway and looked back. "But seriously, read that interview. I want to talk politics with someone with a brain over the age of thirty-five."

"I will," Alan promised, smirking. "After all, it's our conversations that keep you coming back."

"It's what keeps you coming back too, in the end," she said, grinning at the double entendre lurking behind her teeth. "I know Liza doesn't stimulate you in the way you need."

"That's true," he remarked, looking her youthful frame over again. "But neither does that jock you're seeing—Simon, was it?"

"Trent," she corrected, her face suddenly sour. "He doesn't know how to spell brain, nevertheless use his. And that goes for other parts of his anatomy too."

Alan smiled. "I'll have it read by class Wednesday."

Satisfied, Piper turned her back and headed towards the kitchen, mumbling to herself. "What sort of terrorist wears Versace anyway?"

I'll set heaven on fire for you

Bring me the sunset in a cup, and I'll swim the ocean to fetch you the moon.
Man has yet to walk on water, but for you, I would drown trying.
Bring me the sunrise in your hands, and I'll keep it safe in my heart.
Pull in the tides, my love, and bring me the sunrise in a cup, because the sandcastles that curve our path need to be flattened.
When I look down and see only two sets of footprints, we'll both know why.
Take the sheep from their Shepherd and I'll take you to Rome so we can watch it burn from the light I set in heaven.
Our destruction is the only creation I believe in.
Bring me the sunrise in your hands, and I'll bring you the Vatican in an ashtray.
Because it's you that I love, and I love you because I can see you.
We enjoy the trees because the trees are beautiful. The trees are beautiful because they don't need gods.
Bring me the sunset in a cup. It's all I need to worship.

Luster, Norway

The sun sets deeper in a tangerine haze.
In sweet darkened shadows hearts are ablaze
to somber soothing songs.

New light
Stars flutter
A cool breeze blows
Lilac aromas arouse the senses
The musty grass leaves a blanketed flat
where intertwined spindles grasp fluently
Individual breaths
Syncopated
Intensifying.

A coyote sends a husky call
to the moon's coy face
While crickets sing in needled trees
When the rupture cascades through the night
Silence ensue.

New sight
Nightlights
Fireflies dance and mingle
as one resides on a lady's thigh.
Blink.
Horizons anew
A chorus of chickadees chants in harmony
after a snoring prelude
A symbol.

New day
Chapter upon chapter follows this page
just written
Blinding sun
Two bodies lie encompassed
Caressed and soft
as new doves' wings
Together in melodious tones
Simple
An item complete
in simultaneous time.

Cherish the Memories

It's like a train.
Moving forward.
Full steam.
There's no turning back.
Who knows where it's going?
But we know where it's been.
And we keep riding until it stops.

This one is to you.
And to me.
And to every moment we've shared.
Every smile and laugh.
Every frown and tear.
And every memory made with you,
Is a memory to treasure forever.

It's like a roller coaster.
Up and down.
Sharp turns.
There's always a rush.
Who cares if we're scared?
Because we'll save each other.
And we always make it to the end.

For now we go our separate ways.
But you're always in my heart.
The time we spent together will always remain.
The times we danced.
The times we dreamed.
The times we doubted.
We'll always catch each other if we fall.

For now, we say goodbye.
But the days go on.
Now is when we live.
Let's cherish the memories.

The Clock

All I am to you are small gears in your clock. I was part of a certain time, I was what that time was about, and now I am nothing more than a shred of trimmed paper in a scrapbook your mother made you, marked with your name. And there I am, in a stunning dress, made of silk and Egyptian cotton, my arm slipping through yours. Your tuxedo was rough, tangible, the only thing that convinced me that day was real. It was real; the way the punch tasted in my mouth, bitter and cold, as I swallowed down my fears and let your mouth touch mine. You tasted of that bitter punch, and the salt of your nervousness, and I could feel your sweaty hands, and I let myself believe it was all romantic, perfect, charming.

And then I opened my eyes.

I am stricken silent, as the last bell chimes and my time with you is finished. There is nothing more to say. Expiations were in vain, and all that is left to do is to pick up the broken hands and place them in the present, on the ashen face of the clock, reading numbers that make no sense at all.

Minutes, hours, days, turn into years and they are all just a series of numbers that measure how far I am from you and how long it will take before our hands touch once more.

I cannot lie. I will long for that inexplicable, undeserved joy at simultaneous love, that one moment where life is a jigsaw puzzle you've been working on for years, and you finally find the last piece, scraped under a table without remorse. And you pick it up, and that snapping sound it makes as it fits into the last space, that sound defines the rest of your life. Forever.

You'd promised me forever that night, breathing those bitter-scented words into my face, though you knew down in that heart I had grown to love that I was another gear in your clock. I was another number, a number of the series of women you would love, girls your mother would paste in that book she always carried, snipping away at the background in the picture. Cutting out trees and sunlight, until my face was against thick black construction paper, lost in the nothingness of darkness with you; a stranger to me now.

Stimulant Series 5

You ready?

I felt a bead of sweat form from the left side of my forehead and run past my eyebrow down my cheek.

It'll be fine. Trust me.

All I could hear were the screams of mayhem outside. The bead of sweat fell from my face. Everything else sounded so far away but the tiny drop of salt and fear. It hit the ground so suddenly.

Hey! Are you ready?

This is a bad idea.

"Hey! Are you alright?"

Joe's voice. My colleague and friend. We were hired by the United States government to figure out a way to keep soldiers awake for days, even weeks on end. We worked for months and finally perfected an airborne stimulant that would literally erase a person's need for sleep. The idea is to relax the parts of the brain that control pain, laziness, and hunger. Joe assured me that the subject's appetite would decrease, but the brain would still force the body to eat. I had my doubts, but I was his assistant and I trusted him.

"Releasing Stimulant Series 5."

After I pressed the big red button, the chemical made its way into the tiny locked room. Inside were three death row inmates used as test subjects and enough imperishable food to last weeks. We had a camera wired into the room so we could monitor the experiment. None of the subjects had slept for three days, and they were interacting normally. They talked to each other about the crimes they committed and their home lives. Joe became increasingly more excited at each passing day.

"I'm almost ready to call this a success," he told me. I still wasn't sure.

"Maybe we should give it a few more days, just to be safe."

"Alright, we'll give it four more days."

Four more days. We didn't need four more days. When we arrived to work the next morning we noticed the inmates weren't interacting anymore. They stopped eating two days before then. One subject was sitting in a corner and appeared to be crying, but he wasn't making any noise. Another was laying on the ground muttering to himself and smiling, and the third was staring quizzically at the camera. Joe pressed the intercom button and spoke into the microphone.

"How is everything in there?"

The inmate lying down continued to mutter to himself, the one in the corner perked his head up like a lost dog, and the one staring at the camera threw a can of soup at the lens.

"What now?"

"Let's get campus security."

Joe called the security office. They sent one officer. We walked to the door of the room and explained that we were going to let the inmates out for observation.

"We don't want to leave."

"We just need to take some MRI scans, the experiment isn't over."

"Do not open this door!" the inmate shouted back.

Joe, the officer, and I went back into our office to talk about what we should do. We decided to turn off the stimulant and try to remove the subjects in the morning.

"Ok, we're going to remove you for observation," Joe shouted through the door.

The officer from the day before opened the door of the room, Joe and I followed. One inmate was breathing heavily and standing with his back to the door. Blood was running down his arms and forming a puddle on the floor. I turned him around toward us to see that he was chewing on his own flesh that he tore out of his arms. The other two had apparently done the same thing, but bled to death in the process. We led the still living inmate into the campus hospital and strapped him to a bed while an ambulance arrived for the other two.

"Please turn the chemical back on," the subject pleaded. "Please put me back into the room."

"Doctors arrived to mend his wounds, but he fought through his restraints. He let out a scream as his arm broke in half from the force of his own muscular tension on the leather straps. The other arm had enough room to wiggle free and grab Joe's arm, and sink his teeth into it. I took Joe to a different room while the cop took out the subject with a gunshot to the head.

As it turns out, the other two inmates in the room weren't exactly dead. I went back downstairs to see one wandering around with a look of confusion in his eyes and blood running down his chin. A part of me wanted to help him, but my fight or flight response was flight, and I ran.

That's where the pandemonium began. Government funded domestic terrorism. When the experiment went wrong, the only thing they could do was a military quarantine of the entire west coast. The stimulant evolved in the brain and anyone infected stopped sleeping, stopped feeling pain or empathy, and when the brain forced them to eat, they ate anything they could find, including people. The infection had STD-like properties, so a non-lethal bite would spread the infections.

I found refuge, a bomb shelter built by my father who grew up during the Cold War. I regret every back handed comment I made about it, Every once in a while, an infected person would try and break through the door.

Are you ready?

I felt a bead of sweat form at the left side of my forehead, run past my eyebrow and crash on the ground in front of me.

Join us, Ed. It's not so bad.

Joe?

It'll be fine. Trust me.

The sun hit my face before his hand grabbed my shoulder.

"Ed, it's time for your medication."

"Joe?"

"No, Ed, Joe isn't here. Drink this and everything will be fine."

Trust me.

You Are My Heart

You are my heart, the thud of the waves against the sand.
The rush of the wind through the cornfield.
And you, unaware, with the juice of the moon
Gathering on the ends of your hair.

Butterflies linger around your lips, caught in your words
Your eyes taste of toffee and damp earth
Mahogany hands gentle as a chorus on Christmas day

You build is opaque, entirely elusive
Let me be the one guiding light
On the sea of your stomach

Your breath unifies the songs of a thousand kites
When you walk, your feet whisper dances
Fingertips in an endless piano concerto

I crave to wrap my arms around your legs
And together we will fall into the day,
Laughing.

Salt and Pepper

I will buy a sword and start a war.
One action leads to another.
Like the way you shutting the door to your
Honda that day
Led to you driving away,
Not coming back.
Never again.

The night sky is black and violet,
Tastes bland,
Peppered with stars,
Salt in the wound.
The stars were never in my eyes like you said.
But I believed you.

I will buy a sword and start a war.
One action leads to another.
Like the way you snapped my heart
Led to an unplugged cord to my little
Blue telephone, hung it up for the last time,
Not calling back to say sorry.
Never again.

The dawn sky is orange and bloody,
Tastes victorious.
I've made it through the war, and the bloodshed was mine
Once again, peppered the ground we used to call Common.
Salt in the wound.
The sunrise was never in my eyes like you said.
But I believed you.

Sylvia

Daddy ate the days of your youth
With a steely-eyed Fuhrer gaze.
After that, all the prizes:
Mademoiselle, New York, and solitude.

The bell jar rocked shut over your phony smile.
Sunday, they fished you out of the dark heart
Smiling with cracked teeth.

You are the woman reborn three times,
Immortalized,
Grinning Lady Lazarus,
Queen of the dead-insides.

You are the valuable mouth of the unspoken,
Forbidden,
Incorrigible morbidity
That shoved oppression down the stairs.

I Just Don't Know What To Do With Myself

"What are you doing?"

"Drinking."

"It's 11am."

"Alcohol is the enemy of depression and depression doesn't care what time it is."

"Is anyone with you? Misery loves company."

"Misery is too modest to be around people right now"

"What's wrong?"

"Have you ever sunk so low, you thought you couldn't be saved?"

"I dunno man."

"It's like the world turns against you, all hell breaks loose and you're caught between a rock and a hard place, forced to fight with whatever strength you can manage. Your every move is a step closer to survival or your own demise."

"What caused this?"

"I kept looking at old photo albums that I don't own, that had no pictures of me in them. I saw one of the girl I love kissing the boy she loves. I always thought I was more attractive than him, but in this photo, she has the most subtle smile and her eyes are closed in this..way. As if she knew exactly who she was kissing and as long as she was with him she'd never need to talk to another human being."

"And you're another human being."

"Exactly. I could see how his hair gently touched his eye and the look on his face. I saw exactly what she saw in him."

"Well, I..."

"No, you don't understand. There aren't words you could say or anything you could do that would fix this. She's pulling my heartstrings, she's the one who could turn this around."

"I'm sorry."

"It always seems that what you want more than anything, the person or object that would help make everything better, is always just out of reach."

"Dude, just because there's a goalie doesn't mean you can't score."

"Fuck off!"

"Calm down. Seriously, you need to get a handle on yourself."

"Well, you... wait. What?!"

"You think you're the only one. Look, I know this is hard man but I've heard you talk like this before, you made it through. And like, man, you're my best friend but I go through this shit too. It sucks but you have people to help you out."

"But it's never been like this, never hurt this much. I hate being alone and seeing her so happy. I want to give her that. I want to be happy."

"God, you're so fucking predictable."

"Am not!"

"Yes you are. Seriously, I bet two kids blindly writing could write out this entire conversation."

"Good thing that'll never happen."

"Touché."

"Stalker" by CHRIS **VALLE**

MOSTLY, I TRY TO IGNORE HER.
HERO GIRL
I TRY TO KEEP HER TUCKED AWAY IN THE BACK OF MY MIND.

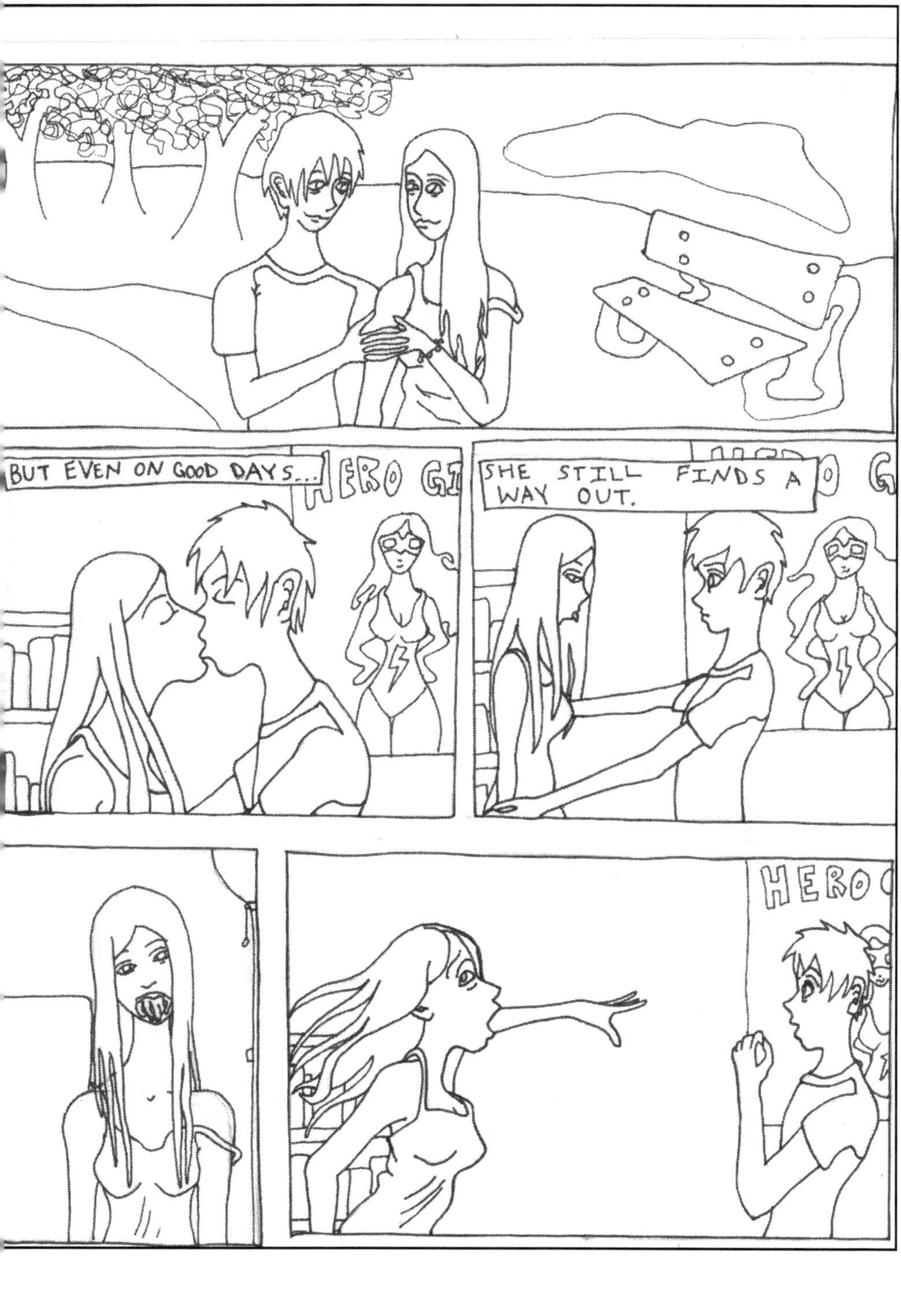
BUT EVEN ON GOOD DAYS...
HERO G
SHE STILL FINDS A WAY OUT.
HERO

SHE RUINS EVERYTHING FOR ME.

Discretion

We can think of several more museums with exhibitions of bodies
in just about every sort of posture.
She told him she didn't care if he stood up straight
as long as he listened to the teacher's words.
He sat down once more, deciding if he'll choose this or not.
But he doesn't. He chooses something else instead.
His dream is to be a serial killer.
Some days he doesn't care if he ends up on the street or in jail.
He flicks the ashes of his cigarette.
They land in her hair and she glares, shaking them off.
He reaches for her, swiping through the air as he misses.
This time she'll move on, turn her back.
This time, she'll leave it all behind.

A Doll Without A Heart

we littered the floor with empty ramen packets and innocence
washing the windows with hard-won sweat and oil paints
too many long nights and too little loves
broken painted canvasses and snapped piano wires
(i wanted you)

we played music for their stereo ears and broke the dynamics
(decrescendo pianissimo)
until the moon frowned
(and we laughed)
falling on crackling leaves
radio sounds washing over our fingers

we taught the world how to use our shades
taking their wishes and making them ours
(i never knew you)
turning them into lovers of the sun
(irresponsible lovers we were)

when i found you there was never resistance
earmuffs and mittens wrapping you up from sorrow
(all too easy)
and your colors were all gray

when i found you with your empty voice
empty shade
(and you couldn't say thank you)
i gave you my warm hands
you didn't answer

so i painted a smile on your little doll face and i called you mine

Terminal Conversations

Flight 564 to Chicago is delayed one hour, the intercom whines loudly. This is not a strange occurrence in the life of Edmond Garrett, at least, not recently. Things are changing. He is running right now, his trench coat has been dipped in mud and valleys and hopes and dreams and is spattered with dust because he slept outside last night.

He takes a seat on a blue plastic chair and realizes next to him is a large, African-American woman in her forties. Her long summery dress billows to the ground, and her thick hair is twisted into a single roll and placed purposefully on the center of her head. She shifts nothing but her eyes toward him, and moves one chair away from him. Edmond realizes he must now smell as though he slept outside last night, and he feels he must offer some sort of explanation. That's what lawyers do. They give explanations, whether it is something people want to hear or not. I apologize for my harsh aroma, Ma'am, he begins, but it's been quite an exhilarating past few days.

The woman snorts.

Edmond continues because he needs to tell someone.

I was just sick of it, you know? I was in my cubicle, typing in figures and looking over court cases (I'malawyeryouknow), and I just couldn't take it. Lying for a living, talking heedlessly and arrogantly about situations I had never been part of. That's what a lawyer does and it sickens me. I was so damn good at it, though, that I was promoted to working on the defensive side of every case. Murder cases. There I was, in a classy business suit that cost more than my own house, trying to convince the entire world that this murderer wasn't really a murderer, and we should let him back into society. That was my job. Letting murderers kill even more people. I let three of them off the hook in the past two years. Since then, they've committed more crimes. One of these criminals even killed another boy. His name was…Christopher, I believe. Christopher Williams. No one blames me for his death. So I decided to blame myself. I left one morning, Tuesday actually, to punish myself for what I did. I left the office without a word, and didn't go to work after that. I had my coat and the clothes on my back, and I left. I do not deserve a penny for the horrible things I've done. I should be homeless now, penniless. My money is stained with blood.

Edmond's words grow thick and passionate. I decided to go back to Chicago, he informs her needlessly. He pauses, wondering if this is all too much for her. I see you're headed there too, he inquires. He is motionless, his thoughts suspended, as he waits for an answer.

She nods, finally turning to face him. Gotta lay flo'ers on my boy's grave, she says. What'd you say your name was?

Edmond looks over. Edmond Garrett, he says quietly, why?

Thought so, the woman mutters. Her eyes take on a sudden blackness as she watches him fidget uncomfortably in his seat. He knew.

I'm Augusta Williams. I used to blame you. I don't know why in hell you're doing all this, she laughs bitterly, but I'm glad someone finally understands justice.

They are both silent for a while. Her biting words hang like ghosts in the air.

Edmond nods belatedly, not sure what else to do. Finally, looking down to avert her intense eyes, he catches the bottom of her plane ticket clutched tightly in her fist. C53. He is C54. We're seat neighbors, he explains.

Dear Chicago

You came at us like a blade between our lungs, and now these ties, these railroad ties, the ties of summer inhalation can't be severed. I alone endure it, the memory of mouthing to her, You can leave me here tonight, words like a glitch in my breath. In the La Salle Street canyon, to which a man wearing a suit showed us the way, I found a sort of god like in the song (you know: early morning, the city breaks, and I've been calling for years. . .) Not a corner, not a crosswalk, but lengths of these stretching toward an end where only cool shadows resounded. This is the philosophy: on every street, there is a businessman to point us toward South La Salle. Let me be the ribs of your lofty structures, my eyes the pinpricks of forked streetlights at dusk, your paths and bustling ambition the traffic of my veins. You are the philosophy. You are my future.

                                  Longing for bigger shoulders,
                                                Nicole

Dear LaSalle Street

sI woke up in the back of a parked car, face to blinding streetlight. You have done a wicked thing; I want it somehow carved in rude, bold words on me: MISS YOU, MISS YOU, MISS YOU. The clock face on the Board of Trade stands stoic, illuminated. It has no answer for me. It is 1 a.m. and I'm stumbling out of the back of a parked car into the middle of the street, blinking at the lights. I didn't ask for this. Remember. You were once a scribbled name on a scrap of paper, and now you are a memory incepted. You were just a series of French-sounding prefixes and a place they chose for films. But it got dark and they lit you up, and it stirred me from the deepest sleep. I don't know what it is about you. I still don't know. I'm walking the center line like a tightrope, HIT ME, HIT ME, I don't care. All I have are a series of images, HIT ME, HIT ME, but there's no one around. There was never anyone but you and your gold-grinning luminosity. There was never any other word but La Salle.

Still lost in the Loop,
Nicole

Rooms

I am a blueprint
that a businessman laid out for you
against other stylish models,
and you bite your nails and spit tobacco on his
Italian leather shoes as you choose,
your irresponsibility and immaturity seeping through
the cracks in your faulty decision.

You will place rooms in my heart, hollow out space,
a room for doubt, adultery, a room for apologies that share a bed with lies
and you will carve into me these hollows,
whispering, "I love you!" in the walls
and "I made the wrong decision" in fresh paint on the door frames,
and burning the house down with
a match that reads 'divorce'.

We will grow old in separate houses with separate people
and your wife will carve out places in your heart,
places that she will never have,
that you will steal from me and give as rented rooms to her.
My name will be faded:
a failed attempt to scrub it harshly from your memory,
but I am there,
echoing "I love you!" in the walls
and "I made the wrong decision" in chipped paint on the door frames.

Smaller Questions with Bigger Answers

ELISABETH ATHAS

    Do you ever wonder what's out there? Don't bother – what's out there will wonder about itself. Wonder what would happen if you hadn't stubbed your toe on that chair. Would you have sat down and made plans? Wonder what would happen if you hadn't slammed your ring finger in the car door. Would you have realized the ring didn't fit even when your finger wasn't swollen? Wonder what would happen if you hadn't gotten that migraine from banging your head on your desk. Would you be less frustrated? Decide to sit down, keep driving, and save yourself the headache. Wonder about the possibilities. Ask yourself the questions while you can still answer them. Maybe what's out there will begin to wonder about you.

Cute as a Button

Buttons started life as many kittens do. His earliest memories were from his stay in the free kitten box at the side of the road. Buttons' daily routine consisted of sleeping in a fluffy kitten pile and participating in a squeaking choir with the other kittens.

As the days passed, Buttons saw his brothers and sisters disappear one by one. They would be lifted from the box, and Buttons would never see them again. As the spring continued, rain would trickle down into the box. The remaining kittens grew quite miserable. Buttons tried to sleep away his own hunger and discomfort, but the sad cries of his suffering siblings often kept him awake.

Buttons was pulled from his slumber one morning, as he was lifted from the box by seven-year-old Kelly. He stretched his grey and white body, and looked around him, the sunlight stinging his young eyes.

"Mommy, I want this one!" Buttons' ears flickered at Kelly's loud voice.

"And you're going to take care of him like you promised?"

"Yes, Mommy! I will! I will!"

Happy to be on his way to a new home, Buttons curled up in Kelly's lap and purred as the minivan traveled across the small town. After a short ride, the van pulled into a driveway. Kelly hopped out, carrying Buttons inside to introduce him to the family. For the next hour, Kelly and her brother, father, and mother sat in a circle around Buttons admiring him.

"Awww, he's a pretty kitty," said the father.

"Look how he covers his eyes when he sleeps. Isn't that cute?" The brother gently stroked the paw that shielded Buttons' eyes from the light.

"You better take good care of this cute, little guy, Kelly," The mother said sternly. "We don't want him to run away like Mittens did."

Buttons' ears perked a little. "Why would a kitty ever want to leave a loving home like this?" He wondered to himself.

"I'll take very good care of him. I'll feed him fresh food everyday, give him clean litter, make him little kitty toys to play with, and cuddle him all the time!" Kelly lifted Buttons up into her arms and carried him into the kitchen.

Buttons circled her legs and meowed gratefully as Kelly set down a saucer of milk for him. "Kelly is the kindest, sweetest person in the whole world.

I love my new home!"

Buttons' first year with Kelly's family was a happy one. The father would feed Buttons scraps of food from his own plate. The mother would praise Buttons for sitting in her lap and cuddling all night. Buttons could impress the brother just by playing with his yo-yo. Kelly would give Buttons treats and comb through his soft fur with a gentle kitty brush everyday.

When Buttons wasn't being pampered by his generous family, he enjoyed sunbathing in the window. The kitten had watched the seasons change from the living room window sill. As he looked out over the snow-covered neighborhood in the late winter, he was very thankful he had a warm home. The outside was so cold, he could feel a chill coming in through the glass. Just as Buttons was about to hop down, he heard a kitty's voice calling from outside.

"I am so cold!" The voice wailed. "I am going to starve to death! Why doesn't anybody love me?"

Buttons' eyes grew large, full of fear and sadness. He wished his family would help the sad kitty outside, but Buttons also feared his family would love him less if there was another kitty around. Deciding to ignore the crying kitty, Buttons shrank away from the window sill.

As much as Buttons tried, he could not shake the guilty feeling that hung over him. Anytime he tried to sleep, all he could think of was the sad kitty's voice. Buttons did not feel comfortable again until spring returned, and he was sure the sad kitty was warm and happy outside.

Buttons woke up to the sound of Kelly's voice as he was napping in the mother's chair one afternoon.

"Guess what I saw when I was walking home from school today, Mommy."

"What did you see, Kelly?"

"I saw a box of free kittens!" Kelly sounded very excited. Buttons sat up nervously.

"Oh, really?" The mother did not sound enthusiastic.

"Can we get another kitty, Mom? Can we?"

"We already have Buttons."

"But, Mom! These kittens were so cute! One was orange with white stripes! One was all grey--"

"We do not need another cat! We have Buttons, Kelly."

Very insecure about this incident, Buttons spent the next few days being as sweet as he could to Kelly, hoping she would remember how much she loved him. Buttons would jump up in Kelly's lap and knead her stomach, but Kelly would shove him away. Buttons would rub up against Kelly's legs lovingly, but Kelly would only yell at him.

On Saturday, Kelly scooped up Buttons and dropped him into a box.

"What's happening?" meowed Buttons.

He cowered a little as he heard the sound of tape sealing the box shut.

"Mom, I'm going to go rollerblade with Sammy!" Kelly announced to her mom as she slipped out the front door with Buttons in the box.

"Oh, okay…" Buttons said to himself nervously. "Kelly is just taking me to see her friend. Maybe she still loves me after all." Buttons wasn't so sure.

After what seemed like much too long of a walk, Buttons was dropped to the ground with a thud.

"Kelly?" He called to his owner. "Kelly!"

Buttons scratched at the roof of his box, but could not break through the tape on the other side. Giving up, he sank down into the bottom of the box and cried.

Buttons spent days hungry and scared, abandoned in a box yet again. The spring rain drenched his cardboard shelter, leaving Buttons wet and cold.

"I miss my family!" Buttons wailed. "I miss my home! Why doesn't Kelly love me anymore?"

Buttons was startled as the top of the box was ripped open.

"Would you quit whining?" An orange cat peered down into the box. "Come out here and eat!"

Buttons quickly tried to perk himself up and look more presentable. He hopped out of the box and followed the orange cat down a brick alley way.

"What's your name?"

"Buttons." His voice cracked with sadness.

"I'm Mittens," the cat replied in a gruff voice.

Mittens led Buttons to the back of the alley where two other cats were gathered next to a dumpster. There was a pile of scraps behind them. The two cats had apparently scavenged a meal from the trash.

"Buttons, meet Fluffy and Stripes."

Stripes did not reply. He simply began to devour the scraps in front of him.

"Hello." Fluffy's voice sounded very familiar. Buttons wondered if he was the sad kitty from wintertime, but he knew better than to ask.

"Well, dig in."

"I don't know." Buttons was hesitant. "I really should be getting back to my family."

Suddenly, the three other kitties erupted into hideous cackles.

Barely able to catch his breath between laughs, Mittens placed a paw on Buttons' shoulder and said, "Let me put it nicely, kitty. Your family doesn't love you anymore."

Buttons lowered his head and a sad, embarrassed tear fell before him. Sniffling a little, he bit at the scraps in front of him, knowing Mittens was probably right.

Buttons learned much about his new friends in the following months. Mittens had several affairs with neighborhood lady kitties, and all of them were about to be mothers. Stripes had terrible nightmares and would cry all through the night. Although most of the alley cats had parasites, Fluffy had the worst case of worms Buttons had ever seen. Although Buttons' new home was not as clean and comfortable as he was used to, he was adjusting, and he forgave his friends for their harsh personalities and many faults.

One night, as they were digging through the trash, Fluffy asked Buttons where he had come from.

"I had a loving home once. My family took very good care of me. But then one day, they just didn't want me anymore."

"Of course they didn't. I'm sure they went out and replaced you with a new cute and cuddly, little kitten the day they dropped you in this alley." Mittens laughed bitterly.

"That's how it goes," said Fluffy. "People always love you when you're new, but once they're bored of you, they simply throw you in the trash."

The kitties dug deeper into the dumpster. Gray clouds were swirling over the alleyway.

Mittens shook his head. "It's going to be a wet night."

Choose Your Reprise

My dear: beloved | sweetie | snuggly poo
I can't: stand it | hide it | live without you
You are: wonderful | lovely | totally buff
I love you: always | forever | more than enough
You make me: shiver | get sweaty | choke on my food
Wish I could: tell you | kiss you | see you in the nude
Your: face | firm abdomen | mole on your nose
Is: thrilling | funny | as sweet as a rose
We should: go steady | get hitched | run far away
If only: for your mom | your dad | it wasn't cliché
I'm so: bewitched | turned on | head over heels
I want to know: your love | your kiss | how your muscle feels
Please circle: yes | no way babe | come back in a year
Love your: admirer | pookie | darling dear

11:14 P.M. Central Standard Time

We were driving home. I had just gotten a new Jeep for my 18th birthday, which had passed by a week before. The stereo blared out 'Cassie' by Flyleaf, the windows were rolled down with the strong breeze whipping our hair all around with the two of us laughing about only God-knows-what. My best friend, Sebastian, whom I call Seb, sat in the passenger seat. He was whining about not being able to drive yet, something I simply rolled my eyes to as I grinned about his childishness.

It all seemed to happen in slow motion. No cars were in sight as we drove along the boulevard around ten that night. Of course, I was surprised when I heard my friend yell out something about a swerving car coming our way. I paused the music, just in time to hear it all: the squeal of the tires against the pavement, the glass shattering as the truck flipped a few times before slamming into a tree. Then nothing, as my heartbeat drowned out the sound of everything around me.

I seemed to zone in and out of consciousness. My head throbbed. Pressure was applied to my shoulders, and I winced in pain. My body ached. There were screams in the distance, but they were nothing I could make out. As I tried to make a sound, I realized no one can hear me. The red and blue and white lights made my eyes burn. A muffled sob escaped my lips, but tears never fell. A shadow appeared above me and I made out lips, a nose, eyes…and all I could understand was, "..stay calm…be okay." Slowly, as I felt myself being hoisted up onto something, my sight faded to black and the screams were gone.

A blinding light was the first thing I saw when I opened my eyes again. Not the kind of light one sees as a portal to new life, but one which makes a person think they stood up too fast. I stumbled, my eyes burning from what felt like dirt. Once I could see, and actually hold myself upright, I examined my surroundings. To my surprise, I was standing on the same stretch of road Seb and I had just been driving, except no one was around. There were no cars, no emergency vehicles… no one. There was no one for me to ask the only question burning in my mind. The feeling of loneliness washed over me as I sank down to a sitting position, leaning against an old, leafless tree.

My thoughts were interrupted by the faint sound of wheels on granite. It echoed on with an accompaniment of pounding footsteps.

"Joe!" I went to respond, but stopped myself and continued to listen, "Stop, no! Where are you taking him?"

The yelling finally ceased when the words turned into a choked cry. Of course, I could tell the voice from anywhere. Seb. He was in such pain. Guilt stricken even. I ran my lean fingers through my dirty, blonde hair as the sounds faded again.

"You doin' alright?"

I looked up to find an older gentlemen staring down at me. The smile on his face gave me a feeling of discomfort, though I knew it was meant to ease my sorrows.

"I've been better," I told him, managing a small, weary grin. He crouched down in front of me, a comical look adorning his face.

"You don't know where you are or why you're here, do you, Joseph?"

"I know the 'where', but the 'why' not so much. How do you know my name?" I questioned, suddenly annoyed.

"It's kind of a requirement when you're in this line of work."

"Line of work? Who are you?" I snapped, my irritation rising.

"Well," he began, "to put it simply, I'm a messenger of God."

"A messenger of God?" I asked with a raised eyebrow.

"Yep," He said, his stupid grin appearing again. Before I responded, I made note of his appearance. He looked a little older than me, maybe early thirties. His slicked back hair was a dark shade of brown, his eyes a vibrant green, and he had a widow's. His clothes consisted of a button-down top, khaki slacks, and a brown trench coat. In my opinion, he really didn't look the type of be "a messenger of God."

"Am I dead?" I questioned quietly.

"Yes. Well, no, not yet, at least."

"What do you mean 'not yet'? Is this funny to you, because I fail to see the humor."

Tears came to my eyes as I thought of dying. I'm only 18; I shouldn't be on my deathbed.

"No, it's not actually." His smiled faltering for the first time, which caused me only to panic more, not less.

"Why are you even here?" I spat.

"I have a proposition for you," I waited for him to continue as I folded my arms furiously, "Either you can go back and live your life, or you can come with me."

I stared at him, my eyes locking with his. He never flinched.

"Seems too easy. You would have just sent me back if there wasn't a catch."

He chuckled, "You always were the quick one."

"What the catch?" I practically yelled.

"Well, if you return, you'll only have a few years left anyway, but if you come with me—"

"Stop," I interrupted, throwing him off guard, "I don't get the point. No matter what, I'm going to die."

He was hesitant in his response, but his smile returned, "Everybody has to die sometime."

With my last nerve shot, I swung at him. He caught my wrist, suddenly livid.

"Fine. Here's the deal: Within a few years you'll have quite the misfortune, including seizures and periods of time where you'll feel nothing but pain. Your spine was damaged during the accident, so you'll undergo several surgeries in order to fix it. The hospital will seem like home after a while," my eyes widened and I tried to jerk my hand away to no avail, "On the other hand, if you continue to stay here, your buddy Sebastien will fall into a depression after blaming himself for not seeing the car soon enough. He'll continue on, attempting and failing at taking his own life for years to come. Eventually, he'll drink himself into a coma; one he'll never wake up from," He dropped my wrist, and flatly added, "It's your classic accident story."

"I have to choose?" I whispered, squeezing my eyes shut.

"Yes."

I opened my eyes and stared into his. There was no expression hidden behind the green orbs, just a blank stare. Had he become immune to feeling guilt simply because of his status?

"If I have to, fine. Okay? But what's the point? I thought God was supposed to have everyone's life planned for them," I growled.

"Yes. He does. But technically, you aren't alive anymore."

The continuous beeping heard from Joe's bed suddenly started to slow. Seb sat up quickly, looking towards his friend. "Doc?" he called. The beeping got slower. "Where's a doctor?" he shouted. A nurse ran over just as the beeping came to a stop. It was replaced with a loud, piercing sound that stabbed at his ears. The team of nurses continued to work on him for a few more minutes, before the five words were spoken, "Time of death: 11:14 P.M."

Eleven Fourteen

"Time of death: 11:14 P.M."

Upon hearing this, Sebastian felt a comforting around his shoulders. He turned to his left, nobody. He turned to his right, nobody. Suddenly the comforting arm turned into crushing realization. Heavy enough to push Seb to his knees and squeeze tears from his eyes. The tears poured from his eyes and collected into a pool of guilt on the hospital floor before him. A pool deep enough for Seb to see his own reflection, but too shallow to drown himself in. Joseph was dead 18, and it was all Sebastian's fault.

If only he'd seen the other car sooner, or better yet grabbed the wheel himself. No, instead Joseph was dead, and Sebastian's not. He really should have grabbed the wheel. The accident replayed in Seb's mind for the next 15 years until he drank enough to numb, but not enough to forget. On the 15 year anniversary of Joseph's death, Sebastian decided it was time to forget. He poured himself drink after drink, until he felt his eyes drift shut. The crushing pain on his shoulders started to lift, and he let himself let go.

Some time later, his eyes opened slowly until he saw an unfamiliar face pierce through his half-awake eyes. Immediately he jumped over the top of his chair. The voice spoke.

"Hello, friend," it said with a smile.

"Friend?" Sebastian replied, "I don't even know you. What are you doing in my house?"

"Oh, come on. You don't recognize me at all?"

Sebastian did recognize him. "No. Who are you?"

Just an entity. A messenger of God's. A master of puppets, some might say."

"God, huh? Tell me, Master, what does your god want with a murderous son of a bitch like me?"

"Murderous!? Not even. Don't you know you're the victim here?" the entity replied.

"Victim?"

"Yes. 15 years ago I offered your friend a choice. Die, and leave you with the guilt, or live in pain so you could live happily."

"So, the pain.. The, the... Weight. On my shoulders. It was... Joseph?" Sebastian asked

"Yeah, right. You think Joseph gives a shit about you? No, he's been perusing paradise, smoking and fucking for 15 years. You're not even a flutter in his heart. He forgot you a long time ago. No, no, the weight you felt... It was me." The entity smiled.

"You?!"

"Don't shoot the messenger, kid."

"You sat around and watched me, no, made me suffer for 15 fucking years?"

"No, well, I mean, yes. But it was at the command of your friend." The entity paused while Sebastian grew angrier. "I know how unfair that seems, so I offer you a choice. Die now in peace, avoid Joseph, and move on..."

"Or?" Sebastian asked

The messenger sighed. "Or we can go back to the hospital room 15 years ago. Joseph will live, and you can sit by his bedside and watch him suffer until he dies. Incidentally, it will be around this time that he dies, too."

Sebastian weighed his options and made his decision.

***

"Clear!"

Sebastian felt a comforting arm around his shoulder. He turned to his left, nobody. He turned to his right...

"Don't worry, son. Your friend will live." a familiar voice told him.

It was the doctor who was operating on Joseph, but Seb could not remember where he heard that voice.

"You know, there's not a more rewarding career than surgery," the man said, "Some live, some die. It's almost like making puppets dance."

A Game Life Plays

To me
Life is a game
That has to be played
But once you cross the line
GAME OVER

Night Walker

Walking through streetlights, seeing shadows in the trees, one particular figure slinks silently into the night past a dark green house. The front porch, wrapping around to the sides, provides good cover as the living room, then the bedroom window looms closer. Tonight was the night, the figure breathed. In a dance with the night, the shadow can see the target now, only a few more steps away and through the glass. Finally all of the research and following has paid off. Assassination is a good business, and always one that calls for precision. I can't afford to let this one live, or worse, realize who I am. It had nearly happened last time. He paused, remembering.

It was a clear night, stars gleaming down like flashlights guiding the way. I could taste the victory, the release of emotions built up inside after planning this night down to the minute. A few steps away from the back door, I knew which window I needed to ease myself inside. No trip of the security alarm, no mess to clean up, I'd be in and out before his microwave finished its cycle. That night, I misjudged, precision lost, frantic I burst from the house, narrowly missing the security switch which I had been so careful to avoid before, and I left that house before the old man could identify me.

He shook his head. He had to try it once more but didn't know how. He didn't need to know- there was only the moon and his keen instinct. He went sniffing for blood, that beautiful, singing blood.

Death and Dinner

At our semi-monthly family dinner, it was accidentaly mentioned that she had died. Grandma's teeth fell out, right in the mashed potatoes. Dad tugged at his tie, uncomfortably chewing his pork tenderloin. But Pam, the endearing little sister she was, went right on babbling in her high-pitched voice, heedless of the reactions around her.

"And after the cremation, we went and bought Lucky Charms at the store," Pam finished and shoveled a bite of peas into her mouth.

I sighed. Enter the onslaught of questions. Of course they were bound to discover the reason for her lengthy absense sooner or later, but I had hoped it wouldn't be while I was around.

"When were we supposed to find out about this exactly?" Aunt Jodie asked, her gaze switching from Dad to me. "You told me she was on a trip to see Venice!"

I shrugged. "She was. There was just a... mishap on the way back."

A chorus of arguments erupted around the table. Pam tugged on my sleeve, distraught about the state of the mashed potatoes.

"What do you mean?" Aunt Jodie's tone threatened dangerously.

"I mean that she was fine until her first day back in the states." I glanced at Dad, trying for a little sympathy. I could tell he was intentionally ignoring my stare. It might have been my fault, but that didn't give him any right to leave me with the questions.

"Well, was it a car accident, a heart attack, head trauma, what?"

I shook my head and pushed away the untouched meat on my plate. At least they didn't notice the tenderloin was undercooked.

"What did she die of?" Aunt Jodie demanded, the legs of her chair screeching across the wood floor as she stood in protest.

"Food poisoning."

Waiting for Harry

Harry is coming over tonight. I should wear something nice.

I slide both closet doors wide open and drag my eyes slowly from left to right. Normally, I just dig an outfit out of the piles of clothes on my floor when I get dressed, but today I make my decision slowly. Someone will be looking at me. I want to dress up a little, but not too over the top. I don't want Harry to think I'm trying too hard.

I pull a few button-up shirts out of the closet, and lay them flat on my bed. I slide a pair of black slacks on, scoping myself out in the mirror as I button them, a little nervous about the extra pounds I put on over the winter. Turning back to the shirts on my bed, I decide to wear the navy blue shirt. Darker colors have always looked better on me. They contrast with my pale skin and light hair well.

As I step into my living room, I try to imagine Harry's voice in my head saying, "Hello, Anna. You look nice today." To be honest, I'm not sure the voice I imagined is really all that accurate. We've only gone out together a few times. Every time I've gone out with Harry, there has been this awkward feeling like we've never talked before. It feels like our relationship starts over with each date. As much as I try to remember anything he's told me about himself, I struggle to recall anything that could branch out into conversation. Sometimes, I feel like he's been asking me the same questions over and over again, too. I am hoping tonight will be different. A dinner at my place is more intimate and personal than eating out. We might finally get to know each other.

I sit down on my tiny couch, and grab my phone off the coffee table in front of me. The digital clock lights up with the time, 4: 30. Harry isn't supposed to show up until six. I barely even know Harry and my entire day is revolving around his arrival tonight. I don't think I'm really obsessing over him as much as I'm obsessing about having something to do. I haven't had a reason to dress up in a while.

When the time finally comes to prepare the meal, I'm actually quite relieved. Cooking will eat up most of the time until Harry arrives, so I won't be sitting around anxious and bored anymore. I open up the refrigerator and take out a package of chicken breasts. I pull a baking sheet out of the cabinet, lemon pepper out of the cupboard, and a knife out of the kitchen drawer. I set everything on the counter in front of me, and preheat the oven. Normally, I am not as organized when I cook, but I feel like putting my best effort into everything today. I feel pretty confident as I shut the chicken in the oven.

Next, I take out everything for the salad. Occasionally stopping to check the chicken, I dice up the cucumber and green pepper. I mix everything together in the bowl, and begin arranging the plates and cutlery on the table. As I do this, I notice that the table is splattered with dried green paint from my pottery projects. I try to wash away the paint with a dish rag and my fingernails, but the paint has been there so long it doesn't peel away at all. I notice more paint spots on the table. This discourages me a little, but I don't let it dampen my mood. I doubt Harry is really going to be inspecting the cleanliness of my table anyways.

The timer on the oven dings, and I remove the chicken. With the salad and entrée finished, I pop two potatoes into the microwave. I look at the clock. I finished cooking just a little early, but I'm sure it won't matter if the food sits out an extra ten minutes or so.

With a little spare time to burn up, I run a comb through my hair again before Harry arrives. As I stand before the bathroom mirror, I am momentarily distracted by the pile of magazines beside the sink. An article's bright green font title, "7 Savory Chicken Dinners" has me second guessing myself, wondering if lemon pepper chicken was just a little too basic for tonight.

At exactly six o' clock, I return to the living room, and rehearse a greeting a few times, trying to decide what tone to use. I quickly decide to end rehearsal, realizing how strange I would seem if Harry were actually able to hear me talking to myself as he walked to my door. By six ten, I reheat our chicken in the microwave, still not alarmed that Harry hasn't shown up. It occurs to me that I might seem desperate if he thinks I've been waiting for him too eagerly. I should try to look busy. I would prefer that he thinks I didn't even notice he was late. Unfortunately, I already have plates of food laid out for us, so appearing unaware of his tardiness will be difficult.

In an attempt to look occupied, I return to the living room and pull one of my writing projects off of the shelf. I take a seat at my desk and set the pencil against the page. At the moment, I'm too nervous to actually write anything, but there are enough words on the page to give the impression that I had been writing for quite a while. Reading and rereading the page in front of me, I wait for Harry's arrival. At 6: 45, I finally lower my gaze as I realize what is happening.

Harry is not coming.

I am surprised I never considered this outcome sooner. I have been so excited to have plans that it didn't even occur to me that I might end up spending another evening alone. I don't want to let this disappointment sink in, though. I push any remaining hopefulness for Harry's arrival out of my head and walk back into the kitchen.

Standing over the table, I stare down at the two plates of food I had prepared with a sigh. The chicken is cold again. I reheat both plates for the third time and sit down at the table. Although I am a little discouraged by the fact that I won't be sharing this meal with anyone, the steaming aroma of the dinner in front of me manages to lift my spirit. I take my first bite, and smile with satisfaction.

"How is it?" I ask with sarcastic friendliness to the empty chair across from me.

"Oh, thank you. There's plenty more if you want it,"

"Can't finish?" I push my empty plate aside, and pull the full plate from "Harry's" seat over to me.

I shovel a second plate of food into my stomach. I eat and eat until I am full and bloated. There is no need to look polite or dainty. With Harry absent, no one is here to judge me.

I set the empty plates of food on the counter next to the sink, and guide my "guest" over to the living room.

With a fake modest tone I gestured towards the unfinished pages of writing on my desk, "Oh, those? They're just some stories I've been working on. I spend most of my free time writing novels."

"Yes, I suppose being a writer does make me a pretty interesting person, doesn't it?"

An hour and a half has passed since Harry was supposed to arrive. I briefly consider calling him, but decide not to. I don't want him to think he is too important to me. I do not expect to receive a call from him anytime soon either.

Left with a few hours to myself before bedtime, I begin shuffling through my movie collection. I flip past all of the romantic films.

I have never been a big fan of romance.

Morning People

Her laugh broke his silence.

"What?" He asked.

"What do you mean what?" she said, still laughing.

"Don't turn this into what-the-definition-of-is-is type of thing. I mean: what?"

"I'm certain I don't know what what means, and I definitely don't know what is is."

"Is is a product of Bill Clinton's stalling, and what is: what is all that laughing about?"

His silence broke her laugh.

"I was laughing before you said what."

"I know. I was asking."

"I told you I don't know what what or is is."

He sipped his coffee, she remained silent.

"What were you laughing about?"

"I don't remember"

His laugh broke her silence.

"What?" she asked

"Nothing."

Her silence broke his laugh.

The Barracks

A light snow dusted the clearing behind our old pine cabin in the woods of Colorado's mountains. Fresh flakes danced and twirled as the wind serenaded them to their resting place. The trees stood sagging under their new blanket as though the outdoors were bundling up for the approaching storm as well. The hazy gray sky surrounded us like the foggy glass of a snow globe, while our cocoa mugs sent up smoke signals in the air.

Above us, cozy rafters creak as the wind tugs at it in a irritating manner while the banister holds tight to the screen. Our cast-off wooden chairs rock silently back and forth as we keep watch for the intrusion. A rumpled rug lay like a canopy, a small figurine representing our fortress as we stay behind our porch railing, out of reach from the adversary.

This night would be a rough one as you and I will lie intertwined like spindles with convoluted thoughts as the winter army sets up barracks outside our home. The lieutenant will sound his windy whistle as the troops knock at the door, pelting their hail sized bullets from every direction, hoping to find the weak pulse that resounds deep within our cavernous quarters. I will guard you with my shield of pillows and the strength of my arms. No harm shall undo our connection tonight.

And the wonder that's keeping the stars apart

hold me like day. sewed
into the curve of your shoe (i live for the harshest colors of your eyelashes)
i make you
girl-ribbons and boy-ribbons;
claustrophobic phosphorescent surfeited aisles:
stitched-up-buttoned-down
for imaginary storms,

and turning the moon into
paltry plastic pearls (the milky way
is too wide a stream to keep
me from you & her)
foolish her and me and you
and foolish gods that play
with gods,

you leave your finger
prints on restless
lips and quiet hearts; the fluttering birds
(we drowned ourselves in her lake)
and you have danced
en tourant, en pas de deux
away from worlds that
shape themselves

for your whims, they live for you and her.

throw me into night; the endless sound
      (if this is what wonder is then i could
        maybe
          sing without you)

To One's Child

Well, son, I'll tell you:
Life for me ain't been no crystal stair.
It's had tacks in it,
And splinters,
And boards torn up,
And places with no carpet on the floor --
Bare.
Well hun,
Life, hasn't been so fun
Turning down the wrong road
You'll find yourself constantly on the run.
Now, I want you to grow up
To be a beautiful, bright young lady,
With a positive head on her shoulders
Chin up, chest out, look forward, not back.
When you walk, don't look like you're "all that."
Now at this moment,
You probly don't want to hear me give you a speech,
But you need to listen up carefully
Because this is something your teachers won't teach.
Now I never really had anyone tell me my rights from wrongs,
I guess that was their way of showing me my life song.
I want you to promise me:
To never let anyone say "you can't do anything"
Whether you want to be an astronaut, a doctor or sing.
Now at this moment,
You probly don't want to hear me give you a speech,
But you need to listen up carefully
Because this is something your teachers won't teach.

Form is a father.

When I looked for form, I found a book with no pictures.
When I looked for my father, I found pictures with no story.
The book was called "My father, Michael." I've never read it.
The pictures were in an album called "Dou , we love you!"
The 'g' fell off long ago, about the time they forgot my name.
The 'we' started to fall off when he stopped taking me on the weekends.
The 'love' was always hard to read,
And the 'you' is surviving without the 'love' of 'we'.
'You' will always remember his name. Even if *you* won't.

CHRIS VALLE

Her

He had
Held her hand
As her belly grew
Into a melon
He had laughed
With her when they
Discovered she could only
See her toes peeking over the
Mound at her center as the weeks
Passed he gently circled his fingertips
Across her plump tummy with a warm
Auburn gaze he traced her round silhouette
Imagining the life that could be encased
Within her soft flesh a child in cozy
Slumber under the skin he rests
His head on every night

Searching for Something More

Beads of terrified perspiration seep through coarse flesh.
Rhythmic pulses disturb metronome heartbeats.
Fault line creases tremble with earth quaking anxiety.
Shattered calluses radiate with guitar string reverberations.

Oh, how a delicate exploration imprints a profound scar,
A scar so magnificent, beauty alone cannot define it.
Burned thoroughly from physical to emotional,
Abandoning an outline of perfect harmony.

Descending into an affection of vulnerability,
The allowance of a simple touch to engrave a passionate wound.
Within your hand, I discover genuine fidelity.
And within your hand, I believe in forever.

The Woods, Honey

I thought we could only move forward, but when I look back I see the same thing: miles of dim wooded path and skin the red of deep summer bark. I have reached a trail marker of solitude in this reminiscence. There is nothing that can be directly conveyed, though again I try.

A letter from camp. The autumn man; I was wrapped around his name like a burnt orange sycamore leaf lazing toward the forest floor. Something peers at us from the underbrush, yellow eyes aflame.

It is 4 a.m. and wolves ravage the trash cans, snarl rustle god-awful thump. The shotgun by the cabin door. Love, Stop, Dear. In a dream he held me in his arms and said something like sunshine, but now I can't sleep for the snapping of teeth.

The woods, honey, they were all we knew: the pines whined lonely, limbs for holding, like arms for holding, the dream where he whispered poison apple truths.

But now the wolves are dead in the road and I lower the shaking shotgun, quivering with tears.

Scent Memory

Some days I worry
the wind will snap
the stems of dried flowers
hanging from my car's rear-view mirror.

Do you remember when
you gave them to me?

Your keen littler sniffer picked them
and your eyes protected them.
Your sacred finger prints placed them.
A reminder of life
and the beauty of death.

Our scent memory
is the strongest of all.
From the very depths of our mind
an aroma lets us taste nostalgia.

So when I smell honey-suckle and lavender,
when I am overwhelmed by wildflowers,
I'll remember the tenor voice
in my "tin can of death."
I'll feel the husky sigh
of your pulse,
and I'll hear nothing.
Because time isn't ticking
until you make a clock.

Dear Monrovia,

Don't tease me. Your heat and your moisture are more than enough. They wrap around me like a sweaty summer embrace. One step out to greet you and I have been overpowered, out-willed. All I want is a taste of your juicy mango dreams, tripping out on our malaria pills. Sticky fingers, overflowing down onto my chin, luscious and full of the flavor I lack. Feel free to greet me anytime, but I can't snap your fingers. Hello. Touching my skin, smelling my hair, groping my prickly legs. These stark contrasts stand between us, but God loves all the little children of the world. Let me serve you, please. Grains in my eyes, and then I see your daughter with the monkey on your hip, swaying side to side on the swing we built. Don't look at me, but feel my presence. Here, I'll help you with the water. I'll pump if you hold the bucket. The tang of cough drops obscures the mission. Waves rattle my breath, I try to avoid the sea urchins. Footsteps reflect on the sunset over the Atlantic. Hold my hand, but I only have two and too little time. Precious dirty hands give me strength to never forget.

>Thinking of you,
>Rachel

Response to "Reading Postures 3"

Capture the spotlight, in day light, at night time as painters imagine a scene to a page, the brush always flowing, cascading, ensuring the pristine qualities of a divine face always glowing, shining as sunlight would on a cloudless day while maybe the engineer or the sculptor may have a different image, using creativity to spark a cause to expound their talent, exude their studies in a glorious entranced manner, if only to bring glory to you as your eyes remind me of the mole hill to your spontaneity, the outer crest of a wave never to crash, for the shore may be too weak at its beauty to keep it safe and instead of catching her, gracefully they would both tumble head over heel like I did for you that night you walked through the door with your elegant grace commanding the room as I watch, mouth agape in a trance, compelled to draw you near, as the night draws the day, you captured the spotlight.

KATIE REVELLE

To Someone Special

there is a sign,
perforating the dried up ocean we call sky
it says under the title of the coffee shop
"GIVE AN EASTER EGG TO SOMEONE SPECIAL"

nothing says love like
giving someone half
the process of conception
hinting like mad that perhaps you'd like to get married
and move into a silver bullet trailer
and have a little girl.

nothing says love like
giving someone a whole
breakfast for one
living with conditions, you're the sort that
colors in the lines and
never shares breakfast.

nothing says love like
giving someone an Easter egg,
making feeble expiations for forgetting
my heart on Valentine's Day
the dye on the egg lets me know you color in the lines
and you'll move into a silver bullet trailer and I'll never be your girl.

there is a card
perforating the dried up egg dye we call beauty
it says under the blue stain of your name,
"TO SOMEONE SPECIAL

Silent Cries

This is crazy,
What I just heard a father touching his daughter
That's pretty absurd. Words rolling off my tongue
Tremble my body, to imagine someone so young
So young, so innocent, can you tell me why
No seems to listen? No one listening, no one aware
That this type of thing happens everywhere.
 How would you feel if this was someone for whom you cared?
Just goes to show life isn't fair or fun,
 If only she had a chance to get up and run.
If you saw this would you call for help or would you stop and stare,
 As if you weren't there? This type of thing often gets ignored,
But in a victim's head is where it's always stored.

I'll Walk You Home

JAMIE BUTTGEN

Walking home alone, the moon shines and stars glisten as a cool breeze blows curly red locks from her face. Her neon orange headphones, attached to a matching iPod, leave her enveloped in a world all her own, untouchable and non-cohesive with the night. Car after car she passes, humming along as she bobs her head and her key ring jingles. Her baggy sweats and favorite hoodie keep her enclosed, a security blanket of sorts. This parking lot divides the surrounding buildings in half, she is alone and invisible; at least so she thinks.

Streetlights spaced yards apart draw her shadow on the pavement below, faint and long at first until gradually enhancing the image as it shrinks and overlaps with a new silhouette as she trudges on.

As she nears the end of the lot an old battered car, typical of any college student, pulls into a spot some ways behind her. She watches the taillights dim over her shoulder as she picks up her speed just a little. After several paces, she glances again and sees nothing.

The song ends.

She is suddenly stumbling, her right hand, which has been poised on her pepper spray in her pocket, tries, scrambling to make it work while she tightens her body and tries to run. No scream escapes her mouth as she flails, eyes scanning, seeing no one around. Her senses altered, she's feeling faint as the tan muscular hand turns her skin white under its grip. The lyrics, "Stop and stare, you think you're movin' but you go nowhere.." play in her ears before the cords are ripped from her ears and her iPod clatters to the ground. She lashes out, every attempt blocked by his weight. As he muffles her cries, he leans her on a silver car as she kicks and twists, hoping to strike anything.

The cold moistened metal of the car beneath her sent chills down her spine as she was able to move less and less. The awkward tormented angle she was forced into limited her options for escape as the rugged figure smashed her hand into the car causing her keys, and only defense, to fall to the ground.

Her cheeks, saturated with tears and mascara streaks, sting from a back handed strike as her head bounces off of the car like a rubber ball. Her feet, snug in black converse shoes, dangle inches from the pavement unable to make the vital connection needed to escape. Her sporadic coughing is rewarded with pain from the silhouettes body that seems to have the upper hand from every direction.

She finally manages a scream, only to have a cologne and sweat soaked handkerchief shoved in her mouth, as she gags and heaves, trying to recompose herself while her body rages out of control.

The next pain she feels through the numbness her body is creating is from her studded belt strap as she feels one of its pins scrape her eye. Her legs are spread to straddle the beast, though she desperately tries to maneuver them in a more ladylike fashion in hopes to prevent the now inevitable. She sobs hysterically as her arms, pinned above her and drained from blood, are numb as she grinds her teeth into the rag still in her mouth.

***

Headlights flash across several vehicles finding a spot near the edge of the large lot. The driver in his cocked flat billed hat, half zipped hoodie and baggy jeans eases himself casually from his car as the lights blink, indicating his doors are now locked. He stretches before shoving his keys in his pocket and adjusting his pants when he sees something near the silver car he parked next to. As he walks around the side of the car he bends down with outstretched hands to grasp a hold of what is lying on the ground. He lifts it up, the neon orange player reflecting some of the light from the nearby streetlamp as he puts the ear bud to his ears and hears, "..and it's not as safe when you're walking alone. I'll walk you home."

There is No Sound

There is no sound so inviting
as the sound of one's name.
A calling in gleeful anticipation
and in greeting.

There is no sound so effortless
as the sound of one's name.
A sweet caress to the body
his satin to her silk.

There is no sound so bittersweet
as the sound of one's name.
Even a black coffee will
taste as golden honey.

There is no sound so fierce
as the sound of one's name.
A stench of weeds and thorns
torn down in the noon sun.

There is no sound so wretched
as the sound of one's name.
A whisper without explanation
after a mumbled goodbye.

There is no sound so abandoned
as the sound of one's name.

Brother, Can I Bum a Light?

"Brother, can I bum a light?"

Glancing up from the pavement, I take in his paunchy, sagging face—his eyes bleary, his wrinkles weary, his back crooked as his ways of making ends meet. I reach into my jacket and watch the split-second tenseness twitch through his face, him wondering if it'd be a lighter I'd be pulling out or a peacemaker.

Click, click, and the flint catches. Sparks flutter, and the smell of butane fills us.

He grunts something in gratitude, and hobbles away to some uninhabited hovel to rest his head. I turn to my brother and light another, suckling the nicotine. As we watch him go, we know there is no rest for people like us.

And now we're in the bar, drinking our sorrows, listening to the blues singer pour out her heart as the bartender pours another round. The bar's dead silent, 'cept her rhinestone-studded voice. She's a young Billie Holiday, with flesh and face to match. All the bars in town are quiet, sad places, 'cept the Irish pubs. Only the Irish drink to be happy.

Our cigarette smoke mingles, saying the words we can't or won't say to each other. The haze stings our eyes, and the vodka burns our throats, but we continue lighting up and shooting shot after shot down the hatch.

"Brother, can I bum a light?"

The freckles and flaming red hair give him away before his temper does, and we watch the scene unfold. He's Irish, that boy, and he's on the wrong side of the town. The heat in the room rises like fat tourists on escalators, and swears form like beads of sweat at the corners of their mouths.

Crash, crash, and a bottle shatters. Big Bill jumps over the counter, and bar stools topple, showing their legs like lady hitchhikers desperate to get out of town. When all is said and done, one of them is broken, but all of them are cheap; they only had two choices in life, them bar stools: be dirty, or be washed up, and Big Bill's too lazy to give them a spit shine.

We look to the blues singer, and fantasize she's more dirty than washed up. Her lilting soprano voice caresses our smoke, not flinching as the plastic paddy is thrown out the door.

"Look at them kids on the corner," Grandpa Leland mutters from the window. "Smoking their cigarettes like they ain't gonna rot their lungs."

"Come away from the window and eat," our mother says as she lays dinner on the table with her mismatched potholders. She's a steak-and-potatoes kind of gal, but keeps her figure somehow. Dad's a steak-and-potatoes man, but he ballooned like our mortgage payments after he turned thirty-five.

After dinner we sneak into the backyard and light up again behind the shed. Toys from our childhood still litter the grass, untouched.

"Brother, can I bum a light?" our kid sister asks.

We take one look at her trying to be tough and laugh, ruffling her hair in turn. "You're too young to be killing yourself with anything other than high fructose corn syrup."

She huffs and puffs and blows our house in, but behind her furrowed brows, she's all toothy grins and chewing gum stains. She looks lonely, playing hopscotch by herself on the sidewalk, so we snuff our butts and join her. Her lilting soprano laugh sends the birds from the criss-crossing telephone wires.

As we watch her, we hope she'll have more options than bar stools. We hope huffing and puffing and blowing remain fairy tales to her.

It's night again, and the bars are all closed. We lay on our backs in the middle of a four-way intersection and stare at the light above us, blinking. We have cigarettes in our hands, and the smoke mingles with the stars we'll never touch—or even see, this far inside the city.

We blink, and the light's gone out.

"Brother, can I bum a light?"

I toss the lighter into the air. It sails and lands with a clatter, clatter. And the stars above twinkle, twinkle, and nursery rhymes grow up and get mean, and instead of lulling us to sleep, they keep us up at night. I stretch towards lights above, yearning, yearning, but find them to be out of reach. I sigh and settle, reaching for my scuffed, discarded lighter a stone's throw distance from where we lay. Before my fingers touch it, I stop and recoil.

"We should quit smoking," I say in the dark.

We blink, and the light's still blinking.

"Yeah, you're probably right."

No One Else Knows

No one else knows
the feeling inside
When I'm alone
in the middle of the night
Because it's your pressure
it keeps me alive

The tear in your eye
strikes something in me
Like shards of metal
that force me to bleed
Because it's the joy
across your face that makes me melt

The grasp I've held to
that keeps you and I
Makes times when you're gone
a heartbreaking crime
Because it's your strength
of your arms that keep me warm.

Snowfield

world that died

"Will I see you again?"
She jumped. "What?"
"Will I see you around? Ever?"
A silence wrapped around them.
Then she spoke.
"I don't know," she whispered.
"I don't think I ever want to see you again."

girl in the world

He drove away carefully in the bright dusk.
She watched him go, mittened hands hanging at her sides.
Snow dusted over her.
If she stood there long enough, she could turn into a statue.

remembers a different world

Inside his house, he turned on the radio.
Thick layers of dust coated everything that held her essence.
He hadn't seen her in years.
"I would have come by sooner," he said, the words naked and cold.
It was almost a lie.

that hadn't yet died

Inside her house, she sat at the kitchen table.
There were grooves in its surface from his metalworking projects.
She traced her fingers over the memory of his hands.
"I don't hate you," she said, but air devoured the words.
Stillness reigned.
there is a boy

Memories of streetlights flickered through his head.
He knew all of the machinations of her youth.
It had been his fault, but at least he could have said something.
At least been there after the crash.
But what fault of his was it for her world being empty?

in this frightening place

She curled into the sheets on her bed and remembered hospital lights.
She could feel the jagged scars on her back.
It had been a long time since he had even spoken her name.
But now he had shown up on her doorstep.
Now he was begging her to save him from the winter.

they will escape someday

He twisted wires together and wondered.
There had to be some way to tape back their portrait.
Even though he'd never been there after everything fell apart.
After the crash.
Before the snow.

by finding the seams in the sky

As the day rose over the winter town, he had a gift for her.
He retraced his way back to her door.
He wondered if she hated him.
And she did.
She pressed her fingers against the cold window and hated.

but the girl has made wings

She heard the knock on her door and knew.
But she would always let him in.
"I told you not to come," she told him.

"I know, but I had to give you this."
He handed her his gift.
She ran her fingers over the wings.

they soar against the deadened sun

"Why?"
"Because I had to make up for it somehow."
"You could never make up for not being there."
"But can't I at least try?"

feathers of the wings fall away

"No. You can't."
She gives the wings back to him.
He steps backwards, almost slipping on the ice.
"I never want to hear from you again."

There is a world that died.
There is a girl in the world.
Sometimes the girl remembers a different world.
A world that hadn't yet died.
There is a boy in the world.
The boy looks at the girl and wonders why she is in this frightening place.
The girl says they will escape someday, as the wind curls around their bodies.
So the boy tries to discover a way out by finding the seams in the sky.
But the girl has made wings and she will show the boy how to fly.
They soar against the deadened sun, but the girl knows something is wrong.
The feathers of the wings fall away, and they crash to the ground.
And the wind curls around their bodies.

The Current, The Lights, and Myself

ELISABETH ATHAS

I remember when I floated
In the fountain from my home.
I bobbled with the current,
And let the lights color my pupils.
That was all that existed.
The current,
The lights,
And myself.
We were simple friends.
In the day, the lights turned off,
And I glittered with the current.
In the night, the lights were brilliant,
And the current whooshed in my ears.
The three of us were destiny,
We were admire and adored.
People came to visit us often,
But we didn't focus on their stares.
It was only the three of us
Because we believed

There is a foundation
For what flows
From the seas above
To the skies below

Then one summer
As the lights replaced
The current's shine,
I skinned my elbows
And the back of my calves.
After all this time,
I never realized there was an edge,
But I had come to it.

It was a place with a ledge
Where people would simply sit.
They might dip their toes in,
If only to feel
The current and the light
Of that young fountain.
To remember that

There is a foundation
For what flows
From the seas above
To the skies below

The people at the edge
Held out their hands to me,
Not for fear that I was drowning,
But for fear that I wasn't.
Some of them jumped
Into the fountain
And grabbed my shoulders.
Others stepped to the side.
They lifted my body
From the current.
They turned my eyes
From the lights.
I remember the smell.
As soon as my ears left the water,
I breathed in deep the chlorine,
The fabrication of chemicals
I'd been floating on.
The people brought me up
To sit on the ledge beside them.
And they said to me

There is a foundation
For what flows
From the seas above
To the skies below

I was told of the dangers
Of the currents and the lights.
I looked into the eyes
Of the people on the ledge.
Some were bloodshot
From staring at the lights.
Others couldn't see
The lights because
They watched the current
Evaporate to clouds
That covered their eyes.
The current looked black.
It was a liquid stone
I could have cracked my skull on
If I tried to float again.
And the lights were dim
To my sight.
A glory beckoning from afar.
From the ledge,
I only felt a breeze
that made my skin itch.
I sat on that ledge
For the longest time
Picking at the scabs on my elbows.

There is a foundation
For what flows
From the seas above
To the skies below

Rebirth the Night to Day

Meet me in the river
and let the tide take us
to a submarine field of
dandelions drizzled with light,
and alight ourselves as
we breathe in the fresh water.

Meet me in the desert
and let our thirst consume us,
let the wind wear us down
to mere humanity
until our only thoughts are
the crackle of dunes shifting
slowly over our bodies
as we become the sand.

Meet me in the tallest tree
right where the tips of the leaves
meet the sun and
we will jump down, down
to the forest floor where
stencils of our bodies mingle
in the musty foliage,
the fallen with the fallen.

Meet me in the deepest cave
and we will extinguish all lights
so only our inhalation
and the echo of earth
can be heard as condensation

above drips onto our
goosebumped skin and we
embrace the darkness.

Meet me in the sunrise
and wear only a strip of
the brightest stained glass
from the highest steeple window
so our colors will dance along
the pastures and clock towers,
and our smiles together will
rebirth the night to day.

This is Cactus Land

We are the hollow men
We are the stuffed men
Leaning together
Headpiece filled with Straw. Alas!
Our dried voices, when
We whisper together
Are quiet and meaningless
As wind in dry grass
Or rats' feet over broken glass
In our dry cellar

This is the song we sing as we till the moldering soil, barehanded. We pour our souls into our brittle cuticle plows, but the land gives us only broken, bleeding nailbeds in return. Beneath a sun that is always setting and never rising we toil, but the earth crumbling in our grasp has nothing left to give. We break our backs beneath the biting, vermillion sun, all willing to wither for a single sprout to live, but every day we end as we begin: barehanded.

Bill Coolridge stands at a precipice, overlooking us with his all-seeing eyes. Opera goggles, dainty and quaint, are out of place in his calloused hands. With a voice as coarse as his burlap clothes he shouts, directing our chorus, necessitating we break the already broken soil. He is the man who cracks the whip in our chain gang. Although he is no better than us, he is King of the Rock, and issues decrees from his outcropping on high. We are the Black-Faced who trudge barefoot through the rocky soil; we are those who know nothing but what is said by the brute strength of our slave driver.

On our hips we carry bags of snails that we plant one by one in our decrepit farmland. The smartest amongst us remembered devouring them today would leave us starving tomorrow—a tomorrow that never comes, for the sun never rises. They remembered that man sows so that the earth would deliver for him to reap, but my brothers have forgotten what it is that they should be sowing.

Beside me slaves Jonathan Wright, the dark-skinned fellow who had taught us to till. He had brains once, but forgot them somewhere along the line. Besides the burlap on his back, the only possession he brought with him here was a compass that spins without end. Besides him slaves Sir Simon Sampson, who swears he can travel at the speed of sound—or at least he could, before he left it all behind. He sings the loudest of us, and digs the deepest holes. The only thing he had with him when he arrived was a queer brogue from some familiar somewhere—none of us remember where any longer.

This is the problem we face in Cactus Land: we have all forgotten who we are and how we got here. Instead of struggling towards remembering, we struggle instead as our brothers struggle: we till the dead soil from when we wake until when we collapse some time later.

Sitting in the mess hall close to collapsing time, we exchange glances and glares. We clutch greedily at our unwashed bowls, even though they contain no broth to warm our weary bones, nor meat to put meat on them. We bogart them and devour the dust within without ever getting full, struggling in vain with every inhale to remember what sustenance tasted like.

We lay down to sleep under the fell of darkness—something wired within us tells us we rest after the sun goes down. Eyes wide open in the barracks, I hear the screech of bunks buckling beneath our weight as we toss and turn the night to day. In the blackest hour, I hear the shuffle of feet on creaking boards as my comrades sneak out of our dilapidated cabins. Though I do not follow them, I know the purpose of their exodus.

Into the fields my fellows go to devour the snails they had planted, none of them looking at each other in the dark, but knowing well that all there is as guilty as he.

And my comrades sing:

In this last of meeting places
We grope together
And avoid speech
Gathered on this beach of the tumid river.

The burlap scratches my chin as I pull my coverlets closer, trying to forget the cold.

When I sleep, I dream of a woman smiling, beckoning me follow her radiance. Bill Coolridge has his funny glasses, Jonathan Wright has his funny compass, and Sir Simon Sampson has his funny voice—but I have her funny, sunny face. Her pale, glittering hand reaches out to me and she says something long-winded and beautiful, but all I hear of it is what I already know.

"—This one has lost his way—"

Lost in this land and as directionless as Jonathan Wright's compass, I toil in the sunset that never rises. I stare over the dark, desert landscape, watching the rays break through the dense, encroaching clouds that lurk on the horizon. Those sparse, roaming beacons tell those who see that there is more to existence than our fruitless travail. But, as I look to my comrades, bent over backwards and forwards, no one glances from their inefficiency. Again my eyes find the searchlights scouring the far-off desert—a flash, and there she is, standing in the light, her smile unreadable. She mouths the words I had not heard in my dream.

"—Isn't it time we bring this one home?—"

And then, as quickly as she appeared, she is gone again.
"Did you see that?" I ask my comrades.
And my comrades sing:

There are no eyes here
In this valley of dying stars
In this hollow valley
The broken jaw of our lost kingdom.

"Don't you know, boy?" says Bill Coolridge, staring at his slaves through his opera goggles. "We lost our eyes long ago."

We choke on dust as night falls again, retching on a diet that gives us no nourishment—retching on a life that exchanges effort for hogwash. We wear our burlap sacks, afraid to shed their painful embrace and be naked in the dawn—the dawn that, in this land, never comes. No matter how queer our voices or magnified our sight, we keep silent and overlook the facts staring us in our faces.

Sightless, unless
The eyes reappear
As the perpetual star

"Spew it any way you wish," I cry. "But we are still being fed the same dirt we walk on!"

Too frightened to do anything on their own, my comrades stare at their bowls and ignore my outburst—and ignore their own ignorance.

It is only after I fall back in line that they open their mouths again.

"This is the dead land," sing my comrades. "This is the Cactus Land."

"This is Cactus Land," says Bill Coolridge. He was a leader, once.

"The people are barely surviving," says Sir Simon Sampson. He was a people's champion, once.

"The skies are always cloudy," says Jonathan Wright. He was an academic, once.

I stare at them, but they see nothing but their dust bowls.

"Cloudy," I say, rising again. "But for a few sun rays."

She stands in the sunbeams, calling me out of my quivering snail shell. My comrades grasp me, and like Jonathan Wright's compass I am pulled in all directions. They are desperate to hold me back, to keep me in the dark, but they only succeed in tearing away my dirty burlap sack, and I am naked in the dawn.

"This is Cactus Land!" they cry from the shadows, afraid to venture from their dank, dark hovels. "We have always been like this—and so shall we always be!"

She is patient, waiting for me as I turn to face who were once my fellow men.

"There was an existence once," I say. "Where Bill Coolridge was an opera star in spite of his inherent roughness, and Jonathan Wright was a man of direction and of purpose in spite of his inherent darkness, and Sir Simon Sampson flew in Her Majesty's military, in spite of his inherent lack of wings. And this existence—it was not here!"

They stare blankly, unable to understand, but I continue. "We had homes and families once—can't you remember that?" My voice breaks, as the soil broke. "Don't you see? There's more to life than snails and dust!"

They recoil, as if I were an unpleasant stench in their floral gardens. "'Life'?" they repeat, then scoff. "What an archaic term!"

And my comrades sing:

In death's dream kingdom
There, the eyes are
Sunlight on a broken column
And voices are
In the wind's singing
More distant and more solemn
Than a fading star.

"This one was lost, Father," she whispers from behind. "But no longer. Isn't it time we bring this one home?"

I turn and grasp her hand like a dying man clutches at life, and I rise into the rising sun.

And my comrades sing:
Those who have crossed
With direct eyes, to death's other Kingdom
Remember us—if at all—not as lost
Violent souls, but only
As the hollow men.
The stuffed men.

It is like this
In death's other kingdom

YEW and I #2

I can't sleep for the snapping of teeth.
All I want is a taste of your juicy mango dreams.
If this is what wonder is,
I am stricken silent.
My sight fades to black and the screams are gone,
Trapped and tormented.

Down Below is not so bad.
Swears form like beads of sweat,
Rhythmic pulses disturb metronome heartbeats,
As the night draws the day
I am awake and alive, but cannot survive.
Maybe I'll get to live in a windmill.